Muhammad Ali

INSPIRATIONS SERIES

Series Editor: Rosemary Goring

An easy-to-read series of books
that introduce people of achievement whose
lives are inspirational.

Other titles in the series:

Robert Burns
Charles Dickens
Bob Dylan
John Lennon
Nelson Mandela
J. K. Rowling
The Williams Sisters

Further titles to follow in 2012

Muhammad Ali

fifteen rounds with the greatest

Hugh MacDonald

ARGYLL✠PUBLISHING

© Hugh MacDonald 2011

Argyll Publishing
Glendaruel
Argyll PA22 3AE
Scotland

www.argyllpublishing.co.uk

The author has asserted his
moral rights.

**British Library Cataloguing-in-
Publication Data.**

**A catalogue record for this
book is available from the
British Library.**

ISBN 978 1 906134 66 2

Printing: Martins the Printers,
Berwick upon Tweed

To Catriona and Alastair. Always.

ACKNOWLEDGEMENTS

The most convincing testimony to the greatness of Muhammad Ali may be the literature he has spawned. I am indebted to a succession of great writers for their thoughts, reports and ideas on Ali, the man and phenomenon. Thomas Hauser's oral biography places the man in a proper context, Hugh McIlvanney's writings were always insightful and regularly darkly humorous and David Remnick resurrected the young Ali in all his brash brilliance. The selected bibliography offers a list of books I recommend heartily. Leon Gast's Oscar-winning *When We Were Kings* provides a wonderful poignant portrait of Ali in his most spectacular hour and must be seen by anyone interested in fighting, Ali or even history.

I also owe a heavy debt to Alastair MacDonald, a boxing scholar, who read the manuscript, made changes and pointed me gently in the right direction. Thanks son.

All the surviving mistakes are, of course, my own work.

Contents

Round 1	Seconds out	9
Round 2	Opening Shots	15
Round 3	Wheels of Fortune	21
Round 4	Striking Gold	28
Round 5	A Professional Life	35
Round 6	Bonnie Dundee	43
Round 7	The First Ogre	50
Round 8	The Malcolm X Factor	58
Round 9	The Army Battle and the Exile	66
Round 10	Joe	74
Round 11	The Second Ogre	82
Round 12	Good Guy, Bad Guy	90
Round 13	Thrilla, Chiller, Killer	97
Round 14	The Long Goodbye	105
Round 15	The Final Round	112
	Bibliography	119

ROUND I

Seconds out

'Man, I was something.'

Muhammad Ali

BUT what precisely was or is Muhammad Ali? He eludes a pigeon hole the way he once danced around a punch. Jerry Izenberg, a journalist who followed Ali, has said: 'There were people who thought Ali was a saint, and obviously he wasn't. And then to others he was the devil incarnate, which he wasn't either.'

So what was he?

There are facts. He was born in Louisville, Kentucky, in 1942 to Cassius Clay, a sign writer, and Odessa Clay, a cook and cleaner. A brother, Rudy, came along later. He was three-time undisputed heavyweight champion of the world. He has been married four times. He has had two names: Cassius Marcellus Clay, his 'slave name', and Muhammad Ali, the name he took when he embraced the Islamic religion.

The rest is mystery, controversy, failing and triumph. Norman Mailer, the celebrated author, declared Ali was 'the very spirit of the twentieth century'. It is a huge claim, so how can it be made and what makes Ali so intriguing to the world far beyond boxing?

Like a coin, there is a double side to Ali. His life has been marked by demonstrations of each side with Ali finally coming up good as he struggles against a Parkinson's-type illness.

Ali shakes, his memory is not great, and he speaks and moves slowly. Some say he has paid the price for boxing. Ali would say he has merely accepted the will of Allah. To the end, there is the double side. The once wonderful athlete is physically frail but spiritually strong.

There are the two sides again. It is the way of Ali. His story is marked with a personality that was baffling in its switches from good to bad, from bad to good. His character was sweet and loving yet could be cruel to those around him. He was brave but was frightened. He was hated and loved. He was both invincible and vulnerable. He was smart and silly. He was once reviled but is now revered.

The following chapters will attempt to tell the story of a man who came from a humble American town and dominated the world by his presence, becoming the most famous face on the planet.

Great writers, including Mailer and David Remnick, have written books on Ali. Hollywood has made films of his life. A documentary of his greatest victory – the triumph over George Foreman in Zaire in 1974 – won an Oscar. Leon Gast's documentary When We Were Kings shows Ali's humanity and mischief.

But the man escapes capture in word or image. Ali, for example, has always been capable of great kind-nesses. The people who worked for him speak of a generous, caring employer. The world rattles to stories of Ali doing significant deeds for people he met just once but found a reason to help. But Ali could also be desperately cruel to opponents, was callously unfaithful as a husband and was capable of being a bully, partic-ularly when he encountered opposition to his views on race.

Ali, too, was a courageous man, but he could be crippled by fear. He took on two ogres in Sonny Liston and George Foreman and toppled them. Yet he trembled as he walked on to a plane. Ali put himself in the hands of Allah every time a jet engine roared.

The Louisville Lip, as he was once known, was also

one of the most hated men on the planet before he became almost universally loved. Ali was a threat to white America. He was an assertive, strong, articulate black man in an era where segregation was rife and discrimination was a matter of course.

Ali's refusal to be drafted into the US Army and to serve in the Vietnam war is now praised by most and seen as a landmark moment in the protest against the conflict. But at the time, Ali was a hated figure. There were death threats, the prospect of prison and harsh words from almost every newspaper in the land.

The fighter who had dedicated every waking hour to taking the world boxing throne was stripped of it in a moment. Ali was seen as unpatriotic, un-American. Yet he lived to become a hero in his country, chosen to light the Olympic torch at Atlanta.

There are also differing views over Ali's intelligence. His critics say he can barely read and that he certainly failed the intelligence test to be admitted into the Army. More perceptive observers declare that intelligence must be weighed on other scales. Ali could be as quick with his tongue as he was with his jab.

He was always witty. Again, that humour once could be scornful and turned on opponents. Now Ali can gently target himself with barbs.

He lived through a revolutionary time in America where old prejudices about race were questioned by a generation of blacks who were tired of being regarded as second-class citizens 100 years after slavery had been abolished. Ali did not ask for his rights, he demanded them. His words were controversial. His actions – particularly when he refused to join the army – cost him millions of dollars. Yet he stuck to his beliefs.

Much has changed in Ali's life. The sleek, beautiful boxer of the early 1960s is now a frail pensioner who naps constantly. The orator who gave tempestuous speeches on the evils of the white man now talks quietly of every human being's right to peace and serenity.

The handsome champion who once wooed every beautiful woman he met now lives quietly and happily with his fourth wife. Ali's life is marked with ups and downs, steps forwards and then backwards. His was never a journey on a straight, true road. But his life can offer every one of us a lesson.

One can be a bully or be bullied. But that can and must be changed. One can be both brave and afraid. One need not be defined by the bad aspects of one's character but these can, indeed must, be challenged. One can be smart at one time and silly almost immediately afterwards. But, like Ali, every one of us can make a tilt at the title of The Greatest, even though we fall short in so many ways.

Muhammad Ali is not perfect. He is a human being. But his flaws and his strengths combine to make him someone whose sporting exploits are beyond the norm but whose humanity can be recognised by most of us.

This is the story of how one man became The Greatest. And how he was educated by life and, perhaps, how his life can educate others.

ROUND 2

Opening Shots

'I always felt like I was born to do something for my people'

Cassius Clay

THE Greatest was born into a world where the colour of his skin was the single most influential factor in his life. He was part of an era in America when a man could be born smart or stupid, ugly or handsome, strong or weak, but much of his fate was in the tone of his skin pigmentation.

Cassius Marcellus Clay – later to be known as the Louisville Lip, The Greatest and Muhammad Ali – came into the world on January 17th, 1942. He was born in Louisville, Kentucky, a southern town that was split by racial divides that were routine at the time. The family name of Cassius Clay came from an abolitionist, that is a man who sought to ban slavery. That fight seemed to have been won after the Civil War between the states of the 1860s, but discrimination lived on.

In the world of Clay, the reality of racism came in the form of silent insults and vicious violence. Clay was brought into a world where his colour demanded he should be second-class. As a 13-year-old, he also realised that to be black was to be a victim. He read about and was appalled by the case of Emmet Till. Young Till left Chicago for a holiday in Money, Mississippi, in 1955. He never returned home. On leaving a shop, he impudently chirruped 'Bye, baby' to a white shop assistant. He was shot and dumped in a river.

Blacks had to mind how they talked, take care where they went. Rudy, brother of the future heavyweight champion, spoke of the trials of the time. 'If we were in the wrong place, white boys would come up to us in a car and say: "Hey n*****, what are you doing here?" But we never got into any fights.' His brother was never a tough kid. 'He wouldn't play football because he thought it was too rough,' said Rudy.

The Clay family lived comfortably. They were never desperately poor. Some have described his upbringing as 'black middle-class'. His mother, Odessa, was a cook and cleaner. She was a devout Christian and preached the virtues of hard work and good living. His father, Clay Senior, was a sign writer who worked and played hard.

Clay Sr was proud of the home he had provided for his family. 'They didn't come out of no ghetto. I raised him on the best street I could,' he said.

The young Clay was a happy, bright child. As a toddler he contentedly wandered around his house muttering GG. As Muhummad Ali, the champ, always said, this was a reference to Golden Gloves, the premier amateur boxing championships in the USA. But he seemed a child of considerable promise in every area. His mum said: 'When he was a child he never stood still. He walked and talked and did everything before time.'

His dad added: 'He was always a talker.' Clay Sr had a favourite story about how his boy had shown early signs of becoming somebody special. 'I'd come home and he'd have about 50 boys on the porch – and this was when he was about eight years old – and he's talking to all of them, addressing them,' he said.

The man who commanded the attention of the world was already demanding an audience. But for all his popularity and his ability to communicate, the young Ali was never an impressive student.

His school career was cut short and was not marked by distinction. Clay became Ali and eventually came under the scrutiny of the Federal Bureau of Investigation. Their files carry the simple and unimpressive details of the champion's schooldays. It states that Clay withdrew from Central High School Louisville in March 1958 and lists his 'poor' grades. In September 1958, he went back to school and graduated in June 1960. He ranked 376 out of a graduating class of 391. His IQ test at this time showed he ranked in the bottom quarter of those who took the examination. Young Clay was never likely to be voted the student most likely to succeed in an academic life.

Part of this may have been down to his early decision to devote himself to boxing but there is also evidence that he was easily distracted and found it impossible to concentrate. His vision, too, was drifting beyond school, beyond certificates to a life of achievement in the ring.

His home life was also difficult. Ali in his early days painted a picture of an idyllic existence in the house in west Louisville. But there were problems. Ali was devoted to his mother. 'She brought us up to love people and treat everybody with kindness.' There were always clean clothes and food on the table.

But Ali's father could sometimes bring trouble home.

Ali and Clay Sr would have problems in later life, particularly when the son embraced Islam. But there were tensions from an early age.

Clay Sr was a restless soul. 'He drank too much and none too wisely,' said one of the townsmen of the time. Clay Sr believed he was a talented painter who was condemned to writing signs for a living. This resentment was regularly treated with alcohol.

And when the father drank, then trouble was not long in following. While Odessa tried to keep a respect-able home with two handsome, clean young sons, the appearance of calm was often shattered by the binges of Clay Sr.

The law had to intervene on several occasions. Clay Sr was found guilty of four reckless driving charges, two disorderly conduct charges, and two of assault and battery. Records show that Odessa also called police on at least three occasions for protection as her drunken husband prowled the house in a threatening manner.

The young Ali witnessed all of this. He saw the mother he loved reduced to distress by a bullying father. He was also confused by a dad who could be loving and generous and then turn into a dangerous, violent tyrant. There was affection, even respect, but it was tarnished by the violence. His father said of Ali: 'He was a good child and he grew up to be a good man.' Ali was always careful in choosing his words when describing his father. The love survived but the pain would take decades to dull.

Ali could not find comfort in school. He was in turmoil at times at home so he needed somewhere to feel safe and valued. He was consoled by the respect he was shown by his friends who admired both his gentleness and the way he could tell stories and keep them amused. But he needed something more.

He needed not just a pastime but a mission.

'When I was growing up too many coloured people thought it was better to be white. And I didn't know what it was but I always felt like I was born to do something for my people,' he said years later. 'When God believes you have more [resources] than others then you have a responsibility to use them right,' he added.

Clay felt he was special but could not yet put his finger on what was his great talent. He was soon to find out.

ROUND 3

Wheels of Fortune

'My dreams started to grow'
                              Cassius Clay

THE world of sport thrives on myths and legend. One of its most powerful stories is that of young Clay and his stolen bike. It is a magical story about how chance can be met with circumstance and produce something great, something lasting. The tale of Clay and his bike has been told so many times that it has been smoothed into something shiny and unchanging. But there are different versions. The best is probably the one that Ali years later told Thomas Hauser for a marvellous oral biography.

The date is October 1954 and young Clay is just 12,

far from boxing and far from being Ali. He has a splendid red and white Schwinn bike and he heads over with a friend to the Columbia Auditorium in Louisville where there is a show, and the future world champion guzzles free popcorn and sweets. He leaves the show and discovers his bike has been stolen.

The story now becomes part of the myth of Ali.

'This kid came down the stairs,' said a policeman, 'and he was crying. Somebody had stolen his new bicycle and, of course, he was very upset about that and wanted to report it to the police.' The speaker was Joe Martin and he ran a boxing club in the bowels of the auditorium. Clay had come to the law but he had also found the person who would introduce him to the sport that would define him as an athlete and allow him to pursue an extraordinary life.

Clay, blubbering and angry, told Martin he was 'going to whup' whoever stole his bike. Martin replied: 'Well, you better learn how to fight before you start challenging people.' Clay made the decision to learn. It is not too much to say that history was changed on that night in a southern town.

Clay started training with both Martin and Fred Stoner. There were stories in later years that Clay was an instant hit, that he was a world beater the first time he laced up his gloves. Martin remembered it differently.

He told Alan Goldstein, the boxing writer on the *Baltimore Sun*: 'If amateur boxers were paid bonuses like baseball players, I don't think Cassius would have received one. He was just ordinary in the first year. But a year later you could see the little smart aleck had potential.'

The young Clay believed he 'fought like a girl'. He had already, though, developed his wonderful sense of humour.

'Only once did I ever see him knocked down,' Martin remembered when talking to Hauser. Clay was fighting an amateur called Willy Moran who was a big puncher. The future boxing legend had been telling everybody in the gym about how he was saving up to buy a scooter. After Moran knocked him down, Clay said to his mentor: 'Mr Martin, which way was that scooter going that hit me?'

But Clay made progress quickly. Within six weeks of joining the gym, he won his first fight on a split decision. After a year, he was attracting the admiration of those outside the little club in Louisville. 'Even as an amateur he had the same reflexes and skills he had later on,' Bob Suerkin, a noted amateur referee, said. 'Usually you see amateurs jump out of harm's way. But Cassius would stand there and just move his head six inches and slide away. I knew this kid had it.'

Others remember Clay as gangly, almost fragile. But, perhaps with the benefit of hindsight, they talk now of how he exuded a sort of specialness. Another boxing coach, Chuck Bodak, said: 'People would stop and look at him and not know what they were looking at.' Clay lost in his first Golden Gloves competition but he made an impression. His bigger, more experienced opponent had overpowered him but most coaches agreed that the potential of the boy from Louisville was obvious.

But would this be enough for him to make it in the brutal, unforgiving world of boxing? Clay had three advantages beyond his undoubted talent. First, he was brave. He never shrank from an opponent, no matter how imposing his rival might be. Clay learned tough lessons in the ring. The Moran knockout was an isolated incident but the young boxer received brutal blows and endured dangerous moments as he learned his sporting trade.

His movements were relaxed, loose and his humour was easy but Clay brought a second advantage to bear. 'He stood out because he had more determination than most lads,' recalled Jimmy Ellis, a friend, sparring partner and future opponent. Clay never drank alcohol, did not smoke and was shy with girls. He was devoted to the gym, his training and his quest to make something of himself.

'The only thing I ever did like drugs was twice I took the cap off a gas tank and smelled the gas, which made me dizzy. Boxing kept me out of trouble.' There was also never any difficulty in convincing Clay to train or push his body to the limit. He was funny, slight but he was grittily focused. No one was going to derail his race to the top.

Boxing also appealed to something deep within Clay. He had a sense of destiny. This had preceded any attempt to box. The Greatest would later recall that when he was eight or nine he would walk out of his house in the middle of the night and 'look up at the sky for an angel or a revelation'. Clay had a sense of his potential to be extraordinary.

'God made us all, but some of us are made special,' he told Hauser. He invoked Einstein, Elvis and the Wright Brothers, the inventors of flying machines, as fellow travellers on the road to eternal fame. This faith in himself is essential if one wants to understand Muhammad Ali and his vision of both himself and his place in history.

When Ali had made millions and won and lost heavyweight titles, he would reminisce by saying: 'When I started boxing all I really wanted was some day to buy my mother and father a house and own a nice big car for myself.'

But Ali was not telling the full truth. He would welcome the money but he spent it with an abandon that underlined the belief that he was in boxing for much more than a nice house or car. Ali, too, stayed in boxing long after the glamour had faded, long after he had earned his top purses and long after he could protect himself properly.

As a young amateur, Clay found something at which he excelled. He discovered something that made him feel superior to other boys. He was special and he knew it. At school, he would pretend the announcements coming over loudspeakers were proclaiming him heavyweight champion of the world. He would draw pictures depicting himself as the champion. When he won fights as an amateur, he would cut reports out of all the newspapers he could find. He told friends that his life would extend far beyond Louisville and that there were no limits to what he could achieve. His excited chattering was mistaken for the bluster of a nervous boy.

But Clay believed. He was not content to be a decent amateur or a workmanlike professional. He wanted to be champion of the world. He wanted to be The Greatest. Clay worked and worked and his ability began to match both his faith in himself and his talent.

'My dreams started to grow,' he said. The next step

on the journey to the top would be paved with Olympic
gold.

ROUND 4
Striking Gold

'I am going to be rich.'

Cassius Clay

A NOTHER step, another legend. Ali often told the tale of how he threw his Olympic gold medal into the water from a bridge. Disillusioned by discrimination, embittered by the continuing racism in his homeland, the story was that Ali hurled the medal he won for his country into a watery grave. It is dramatic, but it is almost certainly not true. Many have claimed to have seen Ali with his medal long after reports circulated of the abrupt departure of the Olympic light-heavyweight medal.

There are, of course, three certainties. The first is

that Ali did win the gold in Rome in 1960. The second is that there was a deep discrimination in the USA that a gold medal could not lift. Third, victory in Rome marked Ali out as a potential champion and a prospect with fabulous earning powers.

Ali was confident of success at the Olympics. His biggest fear was the flying. 'We had a rough flight going to California for the trials,' Joe Martin, his trainer said.

'So when the time came to go to Rome, he said he wasn't going to fly,' said Martin, who calmed him, convining the young contender that the route to the heavyweight championship of the world would be made much smoother by the acquisition of a gold medal.

Ali was much more relaxed about the level of opposition. On a trip to New York in the summer of 1960, shortly before the Olympic Games, the young Clay visited Madison Square Garden, the mecca of the sport. Introduced to the legendary matchmaker, Teddy Brenner, Clay simply said he was going to win gold and would box in the famed arena in the future. He borrowed $10 from Brenner, saying he would pay it back when the gold medal was around his neck.

His faith in himself was bolstered by continued success in amateur tournaments. Clay finished with a remarkable amateur record. He won six Kentucky Golden Gloves titles and two national Golden Gloves championships. Even a mishap such as a loss in the Pan-American Games to left-hander Amos Johnson was brushed aside. Clay always said he learned from defeats, he was never disheartened by them.

On the flight to Rome, he told everyone that would listen that the gold medal was coming back with him. He was certainly in ebullient form in the Olympic Village in Rome in September 1960. He was so popular among other athletes that one said: 'You would have thought he was running for mayor.'

His room mate, Wilbert 'Skeeter' McClure, confirmed Clay was easygoing, funny and warm. But he also talked of how the young boxer worked hard at every facet of his sport. 'He was outgoing but he was seriously into boxing,' said McClure. 'I don't know of anybody in the team who took it more seriously than he did. We'd walk around and he'd go up to people and shake hands with them, but he had his mind on training. He worked hard for that gold medal. He trained very, very hard. He was one of the hardest trainers I have ever seen.'

The first three fights went according to plan, with Clay winning two by unanimous decisions and the third by knockout. Clay faced Zbigniew Pietrzykowski of Poland in the battle for gold. The Pole was experienced and sharp. He had three European Championships and took the bronze medal at the 1956 Olympic Games.

Clay faced a huge test. He struggled in the first two rounds and the destination of the gold seemed to be Poland rather than the USA. Then Clay found the strength, courage and reserves to turn the fight in the third and final round. 'I knew I had to take that round big to win,' he said. A journalist covering the fight reported that Clay 'came close' to knocking out the Pole. The gold medal was his.

But back at home old attitudes could not be changed by Olympic glory. Clay was proud of his achievement. One friend reported that the champion slept with his medal around his neck. He was, though, a second-class citizen in his homeland.

One exchange in a restaurant summed up the brutal reality of the USA in the 1960s. Clay and friends went for a meal only to be told by the manager that they could not be served because of their colour. 'But he's the Olympic champ,' protested his friends. 'I don't give a damn who he is. Get him out of here,' was the reply.

Clay, of course, was aware of discrimination. He had met it all his life. He was cagey when addressing the matter with the press. When questioned on discrimination by a Russian journalist in Rome, Clay replied: 'Tell your readers we have qualified people working on that problem and I am not worried about the outcome. To me, the USA is the best country in the world, including yours.' It was a diplomatic answer but Clay knew it was not the truth.

He was dismayed at what was happening in his homeland and his reception in Rome merely made the USA look primitive. Clay was feted by Italians and knew he could eat anywhere and go where he pleased. He enjoyed the taste of an unusual freedom and was buoyed by his rising fame. His performances in the ring confirmed that he was an extraordinary talent with a bright future. Clay came back to the USA energised and confident. Dick Schaap, an American journalist, remembers walking around Times Square with Clay wearing an Olympic jacket and his gold medal around his neck. He stared at the bright lights and could have been forgiven for believing they shone just for him.

His next move was to turn professional. 'There were a lot of people who wanted to take him over,' said his father. Clay was at the centre of a feeding frenzy with trainers, managers and promoters queuing to make cash off his back. He was a slick, smooth boxer with an entertaining style and a gold medal at the Olympic Games. The boxing business looked at him and just saw dollar signs.

Clay's father had dismissed moves by Joe Martin, his son's first trainer, to take the boxer into the financial arms of William Reynolds, a tobacco millionaire. There were some who argued that Clay Sr did not want to have any more dealings with Martin because the trainer was a white policeman. The older Clay had, after all, run foul of police in Louisville. Others said that the young Clay had worked on the estate of Reynolds as a young boy and had been appalled at the treatment of employees, saying he had been regarded almost as a slave.

The boxer and his family were in a position to choose. There is evidence that the decision was made even before Clay struck gold. 'Skeeter' McClure remembers conversations with his room mate as the Olympic Games went on. 'One day he told me: 'I've got eleven millionaires back in Louisville who are going to put up money for me. I'm going to make them rich and I am going to be rich, and I am going to be heavyweight champion of the world.'

McClure was sceptical. He couldn't believe that such a group could exist. 'In those days no one was putting that kind of money in a fighter's kitty,' he said.

But Clay was about to change all the old certainties about professional boxing. He was one of the first in a line of legends who took gold at the Olympics and then went on to profitable boxing careers. These included his future opponents Joe Frazier and George Foreman.

Clay was about to strike gold in another way. McClure

was at home eating breakfast after the Olympics and looked at his newspaper. 'There he was,' he said. 'Cassius Clay with a roomful of millionaires.' The boxer had been given financial clout. But he now had to back that investment with his exploits in the ring.

ROUND 5

A Professional Life

'The boy needed a good spanking but I wasn't
sure who was going to give it to him.'
Archie Moore, Cassius Clay's first trainer

THE tall man sprinted across the Julia Tuttle
causeway. It was Miami 1960 and every day
seemed to be beautiful. As the sun rose, the figure
wearing black paratrooper boots could be made out
against the skyline.

Cassius Clay was heading to work. 'Many a time I
got a call from police,' said Angelo Dundee, his trainer.
'They asked: "Who's the tall, skinny guy running across
the causeway? He said he is your fighter".'

Dundee vouched for the young man. He had to

because Miami police were deeply suspicious of any black man who was running. This was the era of blatant discrimination and Clay was travelling in from Overend, the black section of the city, to train at the Fifth Street Gym in the white section.

He was taking the first steps to his coronation as king of the boxing world. He was already earning money. The Louisville Group, comprised of eleven white millionaires and overseen by a lawyer, gave Clay a monthly stipend of $333 and a bonus of $10,000 in return for a share of his winnings. 'It was mostly a fun thing,' said a spokesman for the group. The sponsors were all already rich and looked at the Clay project as a sporting bet with no downside. The contract was to run until October 1966.

The group's first move, though, ended in failure. Its choice for the boxer's first trainer was Archie Moore, an experienced and classy fighter. Moore had been light heavyweight champion of the world for ten years. But the partnership between him and Clay never worked. It lasted six, tempestuous weeks.

'He had all the natural talent in the world but was not always willing to learn,' said Moore, who went on to fight his pupil and lose in 1962.

'The boy needed a good spanking but I wasn't sure

who would give it to him,' he added. Clay did not like to be told what to do. He hated being ordered to perform chores such as sweeping the floor or washing up. Clay was used to his mother cleaning up after him. He protested he was at training camp to learn how to become a champion not a maid.

The boxer, though, was then handed to the trainer who was to stay in his corner for the rest of his career. Angelo Dundee was only 37 when he took charge of the prospect, but he was enormously experienced and immediately knew he had to guide Clay rather than order him about.

He had no complaints about the attitude of his new pupil. Clay would sprint up the stairs into a gym that was rough but ready to produce champions. The open windows allowed the merest breath of air to intrude as champions such as Florentina Fernandez and Willie Pastrano went about their work.

Clay was always ready to go to work, too. 'He was a workaholic,' said Dundee. 'He would spend hours in the gym, always the first to arrive, always the last to leave. He was punching the bags, sparring with anyone he could, doing his exercises in front of the gym's floor to ceiling mirror – preening and flicking jabs at imaginary opponents.'

Ferdie Pacheco, who became the boxer's doctor, recalled of the young Clay: 'He was a perfect physical specimen.' And he knew it. There was no false modesty about the young man.

Dundee had met Clay years before in 1957 when the trainer was in Louisville with his world light heavyweight champion, Pastrano. The trainer and fighter were relaxing in their room when reception called to ask if they would speak to a young man. It was Clay. 'There is nothing on the television,' said Pastrano. 'Let the kid come up.' Clay came up and talked for hours, seeking tips and basking in the experience of the older men.

Dundee had kept an eye on the young man and was delighted to be asked to train him. He had his moments with the man who become Muhammad Ali. But they made history together. Dundee always seemed to know the partnership would work. He was soon to discover physical evidence of his instinctive feeling. Even before he broke through to the top rank, Clay had sparred with Pastrano, a world champion, and gave him a boxing lesson. Then Ingemar Johansson – in the country to fight Floyd Patterson for the heavyweight championship of the world in 1961 – sparred with Clay before the fight. The young man outboxed and outfoxed the title contender.

'I'm the one who should be fighting Patterson, not

you,' said Clay in his trademark manner. 'Come and get me sucker.' Johansson could not. It was clear that Clay was going to be a star. But he had to match hard work with his talent. And he did.

Hank Kaplan, the boxing historian, remembered how dedicated the youngster was to boxing. 'He lived a spartan life,' he said. 'He was very clean-living. I remember when I was standing on a street corner in Overtown talking with him and I was about to light a cigarette. He pulled the cigarette out of my mouth and said: "You know you should not be smoking". He pulled a pen out of my pocket and wrote his name on the cigarette. He said: "You keep this. It's going to be worth a lot of money someday".' According to the photographer, Flip Schulke, the cigarette now rests in a museum in Louisville.

Clay's every day was dominated by training. He spent four hours at the gym and then sprinted back to Overtown to spend time with people of his own age. But he slipped off to his room as night fell. 'The hardest part of training,' said Clay, 'is the loneliness. I can't go out on the street at night and mix with people, 'cause they wouldn't be out there if they were up to any good. Here I am surrounded by showgirls, whisky and nobody watching me. All this temptation and me trying to train to be a boxer. It's something to think about.'

But he would not be swayed. 'Now I got the gold medal and I got the car. I'd be plain silly to give in to temptation now when I'm just about to reach out and get the world title.'

But Dundee was not going to rush Clay. His first professional fight was in October 1960 under the tutelage of Moore. Dundee took over for his second fight on December 27th, 1960. He was to fight and beat 18 opponents before he had his chance at the world title in February 1964. The switch to Dundee did not disturb Clay. He had been with his new trainer only a week but he finished the job in four rounds.

His progress to the top seemed straightforward. He was brought down to earth, though, by Lucien 'Sonny' Banks at Madison Square Garden in New York in February 1962. A crunching left hook from the boxer from Detroit left Clay on the canvas. This showed that Clay had much to learn. But it also testified to the youngster's toughness. Aged only 20 and in his eleventh professional fight, Clay rose from the floor to beat Banks in round four. He was making an impression. Jack Dempsey, the famous former world champion, was mesmerised by the words and charisma of Clay. 'I don't care if this kid cannot fight a lick. I am for him.'

But Clay could fight more than a lick. Archie Moore, his first trainer, was almost contemptuously swept aside as Clay racked up his unbeaten record. Doug Jones gave Clay a hard test in March 1963 but the future great won a close decision.

Then came his most sensational fight so far. Clay travelled to London to fight Henry Cooper, the English boxer, in June. The American was dismissive of his opponent. He nearly paid an expensive price for his attitude. As round four drew to a close, Cooper dropped the youngster with his trademark left hook known as 'Enry's 'Ammer. Clay, showing that incredible strength and will that marked his career, rose at the count of four. He was undeniably shaky, though, as he made his way to his corner when the bell rang moments later. The crowd bayed in anticipation, sensing Clay could not come back from such a blow.

He was possibly saved from a humiliating defeat by the actions of Dundee, the craftiest of cornermen. The trainer had spotted a tear in Clay's glove earlier in the fight. Dundee put a finger in the tear, making it bigger. He then drew the damaged glove to the attention of the referee. There was therefore a short delay before the start of the next round. It was more than enough for Clay to recover. He rose from his stool and took just more than a minute to end the fight. An onslaught by the youngster cut Cooper so badly that the bout had to be stopped.

Clay was a step nearer a world championship fight. He had won through talent and tenacity. But he knew he had to thank Dundee for that moment when the trainer used his brains so that Clay could gather his befuddled senses. Clay, though, was now focused. His eyes were on the championship of the world.

ROUND 6

Bonnie Dundee

'He was always there when I needed him.'
Muhammad Ali on Angelo Dundee

CASSIUS Clay changed his name to Muhammad Ali. He gathered an army of hangers-on and helpers. He won and lost world title fights. He was the fastest and then became slow. He was The Greatest and then became beatable.

But when he was fighting, Angelo Dundee was always at his side. 'He was with me from my second profess-ional fight,' said Ali of a relationship that started with the bout against Herb Siler in December 1960 and ended with the loss to Trevor Berbick almost exactly 21 years later. 'And no matter what happened he was always my friend. He never interfered with my personal life. There was no bossing, no telling me what to do or what not to do, in or out of the ring. He was always there when I needed him and he always treated me with respect. There wasn't ever any problem between us.'

This was a result of the genius of the boxing trainer born Angelo Mirena in Philadelphia in 1921. Archie Moore, briefly Ali's first trainer, had tried to tell Ali what to do. Dundee was more clever. He made suggestions, then praised Ali if the changes worked out. He always tried to ensure that Ali thought he was doing it by himself. 'The important thing was to always make him feel he was the guy,' said Dundee. How did he do this? 'You have to combine certain qualities to be a trainer,' said Dundee. 'You have to be a doctor, an engineer, a psychologist, an actor. . .'

So how did Dundee manage to graduate in such an array of professions? He came from a large American-Italian family and left Philadelphia to make a living in boxing. He travelled to New York where he worked with his older brother, Chris, who managed fighters and promoted matches. Angelo was willing to work hard to make a buck. He ran errands, he carried the water bucket, he travelled to out-of-town shows with boxers. All the time he was learning the details of boxing from legendary cornermen.

His choice of Dundee for his second name came as the result of an older brother. This brother took the name so that the Mirena family, most particularly his father, did not know he was fighting professionally. The Dundee name was taken from Johnny Dundee who was a featherweight and junior lightweight boxer who fought from 1910 until 1932. Dundee was born Giuseppe Curreri in Sciacca, Sicily, but was raised in the United States. The Dundee brothers, once the Mirena brothers, adopted his name.

But boxing opportunities were becoming scarce in New York. It was an overcrowded market. Chris and Angelo moved to Miami where they took over the run-down Fifth Street Gym. Angelo achieved great success there, particularly with Willie Pastrano, the world light-heavyweight champion. He also improved other fighters and his reputation was growing. He was an obvious choice to take over when the Archie Moore experiment ended badly.

He took over in December 1969 for $125 a week. This was later renegotiated when Ali had won the world championship and was earning millions. He was the most constant of Ali's companions as The Greatest's retinue slowly grew to resemble a circus. Dundee is the most famous of the Ali sidemen but there was also Ferdie Pacheco, the Miami doctor, who tended to the champion for most of his career before bowing out when he believed Ali was taking too much punishment.

There was also famously Bundini Brown, who had also worked with Sugar Ray Robinson, the legendary middleweight. It was always hard to say precisely what Brown did. He stood in Ali's corner, he carried the bucket and he talked incessantly. He is remembered now as the unsophisticated poet who came up with: 'Floats like a butterfly, stings like a bee.'

Bundini and Ali pioneered a form of rap with their constant, rhythmic dialogue when training and the excruciating poems Ali would devise to deride his opponents. One of the most popular came before Ali's fight with Sonny Liston, the world champion. Ali predicted he would knock the world champion out of the ring and into orbit, ending his poem thus:

> Who would have thought when they came to the fight?
> That they'd witness the launching of a human satellite.
> Yes the crowd did not dream, when they put up the
> money,
> That they would see a total eclipse of the Sonny.

Bundini was one of the most curious of the Ali followers. He was loved by the fighter but was also regularly the butt of Ali's anger. Bundini, a heavy drinker, went on to die a lonely and sad man but his life was peppered with extraordinary moments at the side of Ali. He was given, too, to outlandish flights of fancy. When Ali bought a training camp in Deer Lake in the Pennsylvanian mountains, Bundini spent his afternoon digging holes all over the site. He explained that the camp had once been owned by Al Capone, the notorious Chicago gangster, and Bundini believed there must be treasure buried somewhere on the estate.

Ali learned much from Bundini in how to rhyme and rap but his teacher in courting publicity was Gorgeous George. George Raymond Wagner was a professional wrestler who learned that the louder he talked, the more outrageous the statements he made, the more people came to see him. And the more money he made.

Ali met Gorgeous George on a radio programme. He was stunned by the wrestler's showmanship. Ali was intrigued to learn that although everyone said they hated Gorgeous George it did not stop them buying tickets to see him fight.

Years later Ali remembered the radio show: 'First they asked me about my fight. I can't say I was humble but I wasn't too loud. Then they asked Gorgeous George about a wrestling match he was having in the same arena and he started shouting: "I'll kill him. I'll tear his arm off. If this bum beats me, I will crawl across the ring and cut off my hair, but it's not going to happen because I'm the greatest wrestler in the world." And that's when I decided that I'd never been shy about talking but if I talked even more, there was no telling how much money people would pay to see me.'

Ali learned quickly. As Cassius Clay, he used the same 'crawl across the ring' line before the Liston fight. He was also at his publicity-seeking best when he fought Henry Cooper in London in 1963. He walked out of a radio broadcast when he was interrupted by the interviewer, he stopped traffic in Oxford Street when he took an impromptu walk along the famous London street, and he entered the ring wearing a crimson robe and a crown. Many were outraged by his antics but some were entertained. As Dick Schaap, the broadcaster and writer said: 'It was still more fun being bored by Ali than being fascinated by just about anyone else.'

Ali used these antics to drum up interest in his career. But, tellingly, he never stopped offering great sound bites when he was so famous that his fights sold out routinely. It seemed Ali needed to have an outlet for his imagination, seemed to need something to concentrate on as a fight approached. He loved devising rhymes and coming up with one-liners to demolish his opponents.

But there was substance behind this style. Many looked then at Ali as a loud-mouthed joker who would be silenced by a top-class boxer. Many saw him, too, as lacking the strength and the will to be a champion. Even respected judges thought Ali was too light, did not punch hard enough and kept his hands too low, inviting a good boxer to knock him out.

But Dundee had faith in his boxer. He nurtured him carefully, planting the seeds of good habits in him. He also chose the early matches carefully. Dundee watched every prospective opponent, noting his strengths and weaknesses. Only when the information was fully analysed would the match be made.

'Ali was a great natural talent and he would have been a great champion without me,' said Dundee. This is perhaps true. But it also cannot be denied that Dundee saved Ali on at least two occasions. The first one was when the trainer pointed out the damage to the glove in the Henry Cooper fight in London, thus giving his boxer extra time to recover from a dramatic knockdown.

The second would come when Ali faced the greatest test of his early career. Dundee had carefully taken Ali to a world title fight with Sonny Liston. Ali endured a crisis in that fight but Dundee forced him through.

That story is part of the legend of the Liston fights. Young Cassius Clay was to face an ogre in Liston. How could he defeat such a frightening man? How, indeed, could he even survive a bout with a boxer who was feared by every fighter who stepped into the ring with him?

ROUND 7

The First Ogre

'That was the only time I was scared in the ring.
Liston. First time. Said he was going to kill me.'
Muhammad Ali

HE lay on the bed, wearing only his shorts and T-shirt. The television blared in the corner. Charles 'Sonny' Liston was not watching. He was dead. The scene was Ottawa Drive in Las Vegas. The date was January 6th, 1971 and Liston had been discovered by his wife who had returned from a trip. He may have been dead for days.

He did not look like an ogre. Yet this tragic figure had once been the most feared man in boxing. He had been champion of all the world. He had been the most monstrous of giants. Yet his life had crumbled after two sensational losses to Muhammad Ali.

Liston had briefly basked in the glow of being world champion. His defeats to Ali took him back to the despair of his early life. He was born on May 8th, 1932. Or almost certainly not. Liston came from a poor black family and census records shine no light on a definitive birth date. He was born in Little Rock. Or Pine Bluff. Or Memphis. He mentioned all three in various interviews.

But his poverty was undeniable. His father had 25 children with two women and Liston was sent out to work in the cotton fields as a young boy. His education was minimal. As an adult, Liston had trouble reading and could sign his name only with difficulty. He felt he had to punch and steal his way through life. He moved to the city of St Louis and found trouble.

At 16, he was already on probation for stealing. In 1950, he was sentenced to five years in Missouri State Penitentiary for armed robbery. He did not mind it too much. 'The food is the best I have had,' he said. He discovered boxing in prison, but he found it impossible to break his links with crime. Liston was always mired in his connections to The Mob, as the Mafia was known. He was accused of being a 'leg-breaker' who collected debts on behalf of gangsters.

There was a darkness about Liston but it is imposs-ible not to think of the huge, violent man as a victim. Liston was used. Then abused. He was also the fall guy in two of the most sensational fights of a sensational era in boxing.

The boy with the poverty-stricken childhood, the young adult who spent his time in prison became a man who earned a fine living with his fists. He was fleeced of most of his money as his lack of education told, but he was the cruellest of teachers in the ring. He destroyed opponents. They were lined up. And knocked down.

Even so, he had to wait for his world title fight. The management of champion Floyd Patterson did not want to expose their boxer to the ruthless, brutal power of the man known as the The Big Bear. They were right. Patterson finally convinced his handlers to take the fight. He was knocked out in the first round on September 25th, 1962.

Liston was contracted to fight Patterson in a rematch. Patterson was knocked out in the first round on July 22nd, 1963. The manner of his victories added to Liston's reputation as an ogre. His criminal past, his connections with The Mob, his blunt answers to the press and his brooding presence made him a feared man.

Round 7 – The First Ogre

Even Cassius Clay, soon to be Muhammad Ali, faced the Big Bear with anxiety. 'That was the only time I was scared in the ring. Liston. First time. Said he was going to kill me,' said Ali, recalling the world title fight of February 25th, 1964. It was one of the most dramatic nights in boxing history. It had an extraordinary prelude, too.

Clay was the long outsider with 93% of newspaper writers believing he would lose. Ferdie Pacheco, his doctor, was reported to have scouted the area from the arena in Miami Beach to the nearest hospital. Clay had been fined $2500 for his outbursts at the weigh-in. Many people muttered that he was scared out of his mind. But Clay insisted his performance was deliberate. He wanted Liston to believe he was fighting a madman.

The challenger was, in fact, frightened, but he used that as a fuel. 'It's a lack of faith that makes people scared of challenges and I believed in myself,' he said. But he was aware he was going into unknown territory. 'I'm Christopher Columbus. I believe I'll win. But I believe the world is round and they all believe the world is flat. Maybe I'll fall off the world at the horizon, but I believe the world is round,' he said.

Liston, typically, was more blunt. He said of his fist: 'It's going so far down his throat it'll take a week for me to pull it out again.'

As fight time approached, there were reports on the radio that Clay had fled. But he had turned up early to watch the supporting bouts. His brother Rudy, later to take the Muslim name Rahaman, was preparing to fight. Clay told him: 'After tonight, Rudy, you won't have to fight no more.'

This shows the inner confidence of the young Clay. He fought the fear. He was later to fight through a crisis.

It quickly became clear that the challenger was too quick for Liston. Clay outboxed and outmanoeuvred the older, lumbering champion. Clay was finding Liston with powerful punches and was avoiding almost everything that was thrown at him. But suddenly he was in deep trouble. During the fourth round, Clay began blinking. His sight became blurred. He believed a substance had been smeared on Liston's gloves and that it was blinding him. He staggered back to the corner and told Angelo Dundee: 'Cut the gloves off.'

But Dundee showed his experience. He sent his boxer back into the ring with the instructions to run until the stinging in his eyes wore off. Clay, brave and quick, managed to keep away from the powerful blows Liston was launching.

Slowly the seconds ticked away. Slowly Clay began to see his opponent clearly. The sixth round became a rout. Liston was known as a bully and he was not relishing being on the end of a beating. As the bell to end the round sounded, Liston slumped on his stool and said something to his trainer. It was immediately clear he would not go on. He later blamed a sore shoulder.

As the referee waved a finish to the fight, Clay careered around the ring, finally confronting the press seats with: 'I told you, I told you. I shocked the world. I shocked the world.'

He later screamed: 'I am the king! King of the world.' Liston was more rueful. He had been shocked by the power of his opponent. 'That is not the guy I was supposed to fight, that guy can hit,' he said.

A re-match was agreed in Lewiston, Maine. It was postponed until May 25th, 1965, after Muhammad Ali, now giving up the Clay name publicly, underwent a hernia operation.

That was painful for Ali. It was not good news for Liston. The former champion was becoming older and slower. The fight was over in the first round. Ali floored Liston with a blow that was described as a 'phantom punch'. There was an immediate controversy with some writers saying Liston had taken 'a dive' on orders from his Mob connections. But others said the Ali blow was enough to knock out Liston. The victim agreed. 'I got hit and hurt good,' he said. 'I felt all screwed up.'

But the mystery of Liston remained. Had he been knocked down by a genuine punch? Or had he taken a fall on the orders of his criminal bosses? Or had he just feared being hammered by a boxer who was fast approaching the peak of his powers?

The only certainty was that Ali was now king of the boxing world. And Liston was destined to become a pauper. Liston was now an object of scorn. Only Ali seemed to have kind words for him. 'They have taken all his money away and he's got nothing,' he said in the post-fight press conference. 'I feel really sorry for the man. He is not a bad man.'

Liston fought on but was never taken seriously again as a contender. He drifted towards Las Vegas with his beloved wife, Geraldine. He was rumoured to be working with gangsters in the gambling capital of the world. There were claims he was drinking heavily and taking drugs. But nothing was ever proved. Liston's death remained a mystery. The coroner said death was from natural causes, yet there were illegal drugs in his bloodstream. Police said he had overdosed with drugs. His friends said he never injected himself. Others said he was in trouble with The Mob and may have been given an overdose by his enemies.

There were rows, controversies and conspiracy theories. There always had been for the troubled boxer. But finally, perhaps, Liston was at peace.

ROUND 8

The Malcolm X Factor

'I don't have to be what you want me to be.'
Ali

HOW was Clay moulded into Ali? Why did a young man brought up a Christian decide that he should embrace a new religion and became allied to a sect that much of white America hated, even feared?

What happened to Clay? And how did it make Ali?

His conversion had many stages, but it was rooted in personal experiences. As a boy, the future champion was always aware that there was a gulf between the black man and the white man in America. And the white man seemed to have the better side of the divide.

The murder of Emmett Till, the black 14-year-old whose only offence was to flirt with a white woman, was an early indication to the boy named Cassius that life for people of colour could be unfair, brutally and fatally so.

As he grew, he began to question the way the USA was run and how the black man and woman had to live their lives. The conversion of Ali was almost inevitable as a young, intelligent man searched for ideas to make sense of a turbulent world.

But why did he turn to the Nation of Islam? And what was it?

First, it was a Muslim religion, marked with its own individual theories. It believes that separation from white people is almost inevitable. While many of the black activists were calling for integration – for blacks and whites to eat, travel and live together – the Nation of Islam preachers, particularly Malcolm X, were advocating that the races should not mix.

The Nation of Islam was founded in 1930 by Wallace D. Fard Muhammad. He met Elijah Poole in Detroit and he became Elijah Muhammad, leader of the religion, after Fard mysteriously disappeared in 1933.

Muhammad Ali's conversion to the Nation of Islam probably occurred well before the Liston fight. One theory is that he converted in Miami in 1961. But there is evidence that as Cassius Clay in 1958 the future champion of the world visited a temple in Atlanta when he was in the Georgia city for a tournament. As a schoolboy, he wrote an essay on this visit that caused a storm in the school. Howard Bingham, a loyal and enduring friend to Ali, believes that this convinced the boxer that he was best to keep quiet about his beliefs. At least for the present.

This tendency towards secrecy was blown away by the arrival of Malcolm X on the scene. He was an extraordinary man, and an inspiring speaker. His comments about how the white man oppressed his race and how this should be resisted made him hated by the establishment but worshipped by many of his race.

Ali was in awe of the man.

Malcolm X was born Malcolm Little. His autobiography, written with Alex Haley, is one of the most powerful tracts in twentieth century American history. The book traces Malcolm's poor childhood, the death of his father under the wheels of a tram and his mother's mental health problems. His family was broken up and Malcolm was sent to foster homes. He drifted to a relative's home in Boston and became a shoe shine boy at a dance hall. There he became criminal. Called 'Red' because of his ginger hair, Malcolm sold drugs and burgled homes. When life became too difficult, he switched to Harlem. But it was in Boston that Malcolm was arrested in 1946 and sent to prison. He underwent a conversion to Islam in prison. When he was released, he became a preacher for the Nation of Islam.

Malcolm X wrote in his autobiography: 'I had met Cassius Clay in 1962. He and his brother Rudolph came into the students' luncheonette next door to the Detroit Mosque where Elijah Muhammad was about to speak at a big rally. Every Muslim was impressed by the bearing and obvious genuineness of the handsome pair of prize-winning brothers.'

Malcolm X said that he had never heard of the boxer before that meeting. But a bond was immediately forged. Clay was mesmerised by the articulacy of Malcolm X. His mind was stimulated by the ideas that were being preached. Malcolm X, too, later wrote: 'I liked him.' It was more than that, it was a much deeper affection. They were like very close brothers.

When Clay was preparing to fight Sonny Liston for the first time, Malcolm X travelled down to Miami. It was then that Clay's link with the Nation of Islam became public knowledge. The reaction was severe. There were reports that the fight would be called off if Clay did not condemn the Nation of Islam. But the boxer stood firm.

'My religion is more important to me than any fight,' he said. He was at the centre of a storm, however.

Malcolm X had fallen out with Elijah Muhammad. There were reports that the leader of the Nation of Islam was having affairs with young women and Malcolm X believed he was a hypocrite. Malcolm X had also caused controversy after the assassination of President John Kennedy when he spoke of 'chickens coming home to roost'. He was suspended from preaching and the row between him and Elijah Muhammad would only be ended by a murder.

But Malcolm X influenced the young Clay. The boxer caused outrage when he said blacks should live separately from whites. 'I don't want to force myself on people who don't want me,' he said. 'Integration is wrong. White people do not want integration.'

The boxer, though, was changing. He saw that his position as champion of the world gave him an influence. The two previous champions had fitted the white man's stereotype of the black man. Floyd Patterson was the 'good' black man: polite, deferential, only dangerous in the ring. Sonny Liston was the 'bad' black man: a bully, a thief, a thug. These, of course, were gross distortions of two complex personalities. But it is how they were portrayed in print.

Clay, now on the brink of becoming Ali, did not want

to be squeezed into either the 'good' or 'bad' box. 'I had to prove I could be a new kind of black man,' he said. 'Now I have learned to accept my own people and be myself.'

The change was made clear after the first Liston fight. Clay had won but the press was obsessed over whether he was a member of the Nation of Islam. Clay was defiant. 'I'm not a Christian any more,' he said. 'I know where I am going and I know the truth.'

He then added the words that came to define him as a black man who would not be moulded by the establishment: 'I don't have to be what you want me to be. I'm free to be what I want.'

The next morning he released a statement saying he was a member of the Nation of Islam. He then changed his name briefly to Cassius X Clay. He believed Cassius Clay was his 'slave name'. The X represented the black American's lost African heritage.

Immediately the world champion was caught up in the dangerous politics of the Nation of Islam as Elijah Muhammad sought to exile Malcolm X. Elijah Muhammad, who had previously expressed severe distaste for boxing, brought Cassius X into the centre of the fold. He gave the champion a new name, one of the religion's highest honours. He called him Muhammad Ali: 'one who is worthy of praise'.

This allied Muhammad Ali to Elijah Muhammad. Malcolm X was left out in the cold. He resigned from the Nation of Islam. 'Internal differences forced me out,' he said. Muhammad Ali said of his one-time confidant: 'I don't want to talk about him anymore.'

The swift denunciation of his former friend shocked many but not Malcolm X. He was saddened but not angered by Ali's words. He had bigger worries. Malcolm X now freely admitted his life was in danger. In his autobiography, he states several times that he did not expect to live long. He was right. On February 21st, 1965, Malcolm X was speaking at the Audubon Ballroom in Manhattan, New York. A small disturbance broke out and his bodyguards moved toward the scene. A man with a shotgun then approached Malcolm X and shot him in the chest. Two others moved out of the crowd and shot the preacher sixteen times with pistols. Malcolm X died later in hospital. Three members of the Nation of Islam were convicted of his killing. Elijah Muhammad died of congestive heart failure on February 25th, 1975 at the age of 77.

Ali's stance on integration and on white people softened over the years. He converted to Sufism, a branch of Islam. His language was to become less militant, more peaceful. But he had no regrets about his conversion from Cassius Marcellus Clay to Muhammad

Ali. 'I'm not apologising for what I believed. I'm wiser now but so are a lot of other people.' He was speaking quietly as he looked back on his life.

This life was to have a sensational, pivotal moment. It followed his conversion to the Nation of Islam. Cassius Clay had taken on the boxing world and won. Muhammad Ali was now going to take on the United States of America. It was a battle that defined an age.

ROUND 9

The Army Battle
and the Exile

'I ain't got no quarrel with them Vietcong.'
Muhammad Ali

THE Greatest was hit with a one-two after his public conversion to the Nation of Islam. The World Boxing Association said it was stripping Ali of his title because of 'conduct detrimental to the best interests of boxing.' Ali's vocal support of his new religion was causing fear and alarm. The other blow came from the US government. Its move was to test Ali, make him a hate figure and send him into exile.

The day after Ali announced his conversion, Edgar

Hoover, head of the Federal Bureau of Investigation (FBI), ordered an inquiry into the boxer's draft status. America was fighting a war in Vietnam in South-East Asia. The draft was a system whereby young men were called up to be sent into action if they passed mental and physical tests.

Ali was first tested in Louisville in 1960. He failed the mental aptitude test with a very low score. 'I said I was The Greatest, not the smartest,' he said ruefully.

But the government was determined to enlist Ali and take him away from the Nation of Islam and America for two years. The pass mark for the intelligence test was lowered and suddenly Ali was considered eligible to fight the Vietcong, the guerrilla army in Vietnam fighting the United States. But Ali was standing firm.

'I ain't got no quarrel with them Vietcong,' he said. 'It was the moment for Ali,' said the journalist Robert Lipsyte to whom the champion gave the quote. Ali's life was about to change dramatically.

'Why should they ask me to put on a uniform and go 10,000 miles from here and drop bombs and bullets on brown people in Vietnam while so-called Negro people in Louisville are treated like dogs,' he said.

The showdown was now inevitable. He was ordered to report for induction at the local board on the third floor of 701 San Jacinto Street, Houston, Texas, on April 28th, 1967 at 8am. It was to be a significant moment in the history of the protest against the Vietnam War.

It was a dramatic day for Ali. He knew what faced him if he refused to go into the army. 'I want to know what is right, what'll look good in history. I'm being tested by Allah. I'm giving up my title. I'm giving up my wealth, maybe my future. Many great men have been tested for their religious belief. If I pass this test, I will come out stronger than ever,' he said.

Ali entered the room in San Jacinto Street with 45 other potential recruits. An army officer took a roll call then split the men into groups to take the physical test. After being examined by doctors, Ali and the other young men assembled in a small room where Lieutenant Steven S Dunkley was to conduct the induction ceremony.

He shouted: 'Attention.' Then he read a statement. 'You are about to be inducted into the Armed Forces of the United States, in the Army, the Navy, or the Air Force or the Marine Corps, as indicated by the service announced following your name when called. You will take one step forward as your name and service are called and such step will constitute your induction into the Armed Forces indicated.'

Names were called. Then Dunkley shouted: 'Cassius Clay – Army.' Ali did not move.

The other recruits were ordered out of the room and Ali was taken to an office where he was asked if he knew the consequences of what he had done. He was told he would almost certainly be jailed. Attempts were made to persuade him to change his mind. Ali would not budge. He was asked for a statement to explain his position.

'I refuse to be inducted into the armed forces of the United States because I claim to be exempt as a minister of the religion of Islam,' Ali wrote on a piece of paper.

The backlash was ferocious. Ali is a much loved figure now but he was, frankly, hated by much of America after his refusal to go into the army. He went on trial for refusing to be inducted. He was found guilty and sentenced to five years in prison and given a $10,000 fine. His passport was confiscated. He remained free on appeal, however. Ali challenged the decision through the courts. In June 1971, he was finally vindicated by the Supreme Court of the United States who dismissed his conviction.

Ali never went to jail for refusing to join the Army. Curiously, the only time he spent in prison was in December 1968 in Dade County, Florida, for driving without proper insurance. But he was punished for refusing to join the army in other ways.

He became a target for severe abuse. The tide against the Vietnam War eventually turned and Ali became a hero of the protest movement. But for years he was treated like a traitor. His worst punishment was the fact that he did not fight for three and a half years and his title was stripped from him.

'It cost Ali a lot,' said Gordon Davidson, a lawyer for the Louisville group of sponsors. 'This was a real point of principle for him and he wasn't going to make it easy on himself. He created this sense of himself and he stuck to it.'

Ali had a simple verdict on his trials. 'Some people thought I was a hero. Some people thought what I did was wrong,' he said. 'But I did everything according to my conscience. I wasn't trying to be a leader. I just wanted to be free. I was determined to be one n***** that the white man did not get.'

He knew what he was leaving behind as he stepped not into the army but an uncertain future. 'I could make millions if I led my people the wrong way, to something I know is wrong. So now I have to make a decision. Step into a billion dollars and denounce my people or step into poverty and teach them the truth. Damn the money. Damn the heavyweight championship. I will die before I sell out my people for the white man's money.'

'Ali was suddenly without a way to earn a living,' said Dundee. 'His legal bills for appealing his conviction were bleeding him dry.' Yet Ali continued to send money home to his parents. 'He refused to carry a beggar's cup,' said Dundee.

So how could Ali make money? He appeared in theatre in New York in a play called 'Buck White'. He canvassed unsuccessfully for the lead role in 'Heaven Can Wait' but the part went to Warren Beatty. His only fight was a computerised version with the great, retired champion Rocky Marciano. Masses of data were fed into a computer that came up with a series of results to the fight. The version televised showed Ali losing.

He was absolutely broke. Friends said that sometimes he had no money to buy petrol for his Cadillac. He sold his tour bus. He was saved by the lecture circuit. Ali visited universities and gave speeches. He was paid $1500 for every speech. His most famous quote at the time was: 'Talking is easier than fighting.' He was good at both.

Ali enjoyed the verbal bouts with students. He did not enjoy clashing with Elijah Muhammad, however. Asked on television if he would ever consider a return to boxing, Ali said: 'Yeah, I would go back.' The Nation of Islam immediately suspended him for 'acting the fool'.

The accusation seemed to be he was putting money before Allah. Ali was stunned and saddened.

But his exile from boxing was nearing an end. The climate in America was changing. More and more were agreeing with Ali's stance against the Vietnam War as pictures and reports of atrocities began appearing in the newspapers.

It was now possible to envisage Ali fighting again. His first fight back – against Jerry Quarry in Atlanta, Georgia, on October 26th, 1970 – caused a sensation. Ali said before the fight: 'I am not just fighting one man. I'm fighting a lot of men, showing them here is one man they could not conquer. Lose this one and it will not just be a loss to me. So many millions of faces through-out the world will be sad. They'll feel like they have been defeated. If I lose, for the rest of my life I won't be free. I'll have to listen to all this about how I was a bum, how I joined the wrong movement. I'm fighting for my freedom.'

After 43 months out of boxing, Ali defeated Quarry in three rounds. Everyone joined the clamour to say The Greatest was back.

But his wily trainer knew that the exile from the ring had taken its toll. 'He was not the Ali of old,' said Angelo Dundee. 'His frame had been thickened by age and his brilliant moves diminished by his three and a half year layoff.' This was inevitable.

But Dundee's final reflection was dramatic. He reckoned the ban had robbed Ali of his greatest boxing years and the world of the chance to see him at his peak.

'We never saw the best of Muhammad Ali,' he said. The world was, though, about to see Ali at his most defiant in the ring.

ROUND 10

Joe

'He just a warrior.'
Gypsy Joe, a sometime boxer, on Joe Frazier

JOE. Three little letters. Three massive fights. One astonishing rivalry that has lasted decades, and may never end.

Joe. The toughest opponent Muhammad Ali ever faced.

Joe. The boxer who beat Ali in what was called The Fight of the Century.

Joe. The fighter who almost joined Ali in a death pact in Manila.

The story of Ali is defined by his contests with Smokin' Joe Frazier. There were three of them and Ali lost the first, won the other two. Joe Frazier and Muhammad Ali seemed to be made to be friends not enemies. Both were Southerners, both were successful amateurs, both were Olympic gold medallists, both became heavyweight champion of the world.

But Frazier cannot say Ali's name without bitterness. Ali, too, is remorseful about the way he treated an honourable opponent outside the ring.

A sense of destiny seemed to force the two to collide and to be first friends, then acquaintances and finally enemies. Frazier was born in poverty in South Carolina on January 12th, 1944, the last of eleven children. Life was hard.

'I was never little or played little,' said Frazier. He worked in the fields at an early age and found almost no time for carefree pastimes. In search of a better life, he left for Brooklyn aged 15 and then moved to Philadelphia two years later.

He was tough, committed and found boxing a sport that suited his temperament and his ability to soak up pain. In many ways he was the inspiration for the 'Rocky' films. Frazier ran up the steps to the Philadelphia Museum of Art, as part of his training regimen, but without a soaring soundtrack. He punched the frozen carcasses of animals in his job at an abattoir. Both scenes were used in 'Rocky' with Sylvester Stallone the aspiring boxer. 'But he never paid me for none of my past. I only got paid for a walk-on part. Rocky is a sad story for me,' said Frazier.

Frazier, though, rose as a boxer. He won the heavy-weight gold medal in Tokyo in 1964 and he and Ali seemed to be the perfect match-up for boxing fans. Frazier, tough and relatively small, used power and a relentless punching strategy. Ali was the fleet-footed, stylish entertainer. There was money to be made in putting them together.

But the fight had to wait. Ali was in exile when Frazier became champion of the world, taking the belt that had been stripped from Ali by the authorities.

Even so, Ali had no bad feeling towards Frazier. Ali told him: 'Stay healthy, Joe. I'll be back.' They met during the exile with Ali and Frazier taking a trip to New York by car. There are also stories that Frazier helped out the former champion who was having difficulty earning a living now that boxing had been taken away from him. Smokin' Joe even started a petition to the president of the USA so that Ali's boxing ban could be lifted.

Something changed. Nobody knows for sure what caused it, but it forced a coolness into the relationship between the two great boxers. And then it erupted in a murderous hatred.

As soon as Ali regained his boxing licence, there was a clamour for him to face Frazier. Ali fought Jerry Quarry and then Oscar Bonavena and then the match was made with Frazier. The boxers shared a $5m purse equally and had a share too of the revenues from showing the fight in cinemas. It was The Fight of the Century, with huge sums being made on merchandising, but it became a genuine grudge match in the ring.

Ali had taunted Frazier with jibes of Uncle Tom. This is one of the worst insults one can make to a proud black man. It suggests that the target bows before the white man, becoming his unquestioning servant. Uncle Tom was the title character in a sentimental novel by Harriet Beecher Stowe, a bestseller written in the mid nineteenth century. Uncle Tom's soft, accepting ways became hated by many who had not even read the book.

Frazier, brave and strong-willed, was never an Uncle Tom. The label made him angry, hurt his family and made his children cry. 'He doesn't care how much it hurts my kids,' Frazier lamented of Ali's taunts. These included calling Frazier ugly and stupid: 'Joe Frazier should give his face to the Wildlife Fund. He's so ugly blind men go the other way.'

There were those who suggested that Ali was only

raising some hype to sell tickets. But the bout was a sell-out. The ticket touts were making a fortune. The truth is that Ali had overstepped the mark. He had a capacity for cruelty and this was painfully evident in his treatment of Frazier.

The champion, though, responded strongly to Ali's taunts. 'He's no martyr,' he said of his opponent's decision not to enlist in the army. 'He uses his blackness to kick up a stir, get people excited, convince people of something, then he's gone. He thinks no hurt has been left behind.'

The insults were traded until both men walked into the ring on March 8th, 1971, at Madison Square Garden. The arena was packed. Frank Sinatra was taking photographs for *Life* magazine. The front row seats were full of movie stars and great sportsmen. Cinemas all over the world were carrying live coverage of the fight. It was a definitive moment for both boxers.

Yank Durham, Frazier's trainer, was extraordinarily proud of his protegé. He told Frazier: 'Well, we're here. I want you to know what you've done, boy. There will never be another Joe Frazier. They all laughed but you got us here. There is not another human being who ever lived that I want to send out there.'

Ali was excited, but content. He told reporters before the bout: 'I feel good. I have never lost a fight when the odds are against me.' And the odds were against him.

He had spent three and a half years outside the ring and Frazier was powerful, with fists that hit with the force and rapidity of blurring pistons. He was also sure he could beat Ali.

The bout began in a blur of action, a roar of noise. Ali recalled: 'I heard that familiar sound from a crowd when a fight starts, the eager roar of the crowd calling for blood. I've heard it since I was 12, it sends chills through me each time it comes.' Ali knew that the atmosphere helped force both boxers on to a brutal fate, 'to die out there if we have to'.

Nobody died, but Ali was defeated. Fifteen rounds of punishing boxing ended with a unanimous decision for Frazier. Ali was knocked down in the 15th round. Smokin' Joe's famous left hook laid Ali low. The Greatest explained: 'The punch exploded against my head and I don't remember going down. I only remember being down.'

Arthur Mercante, the referee, called it the 'most vicious fight' he had ever seen. The action was relentless and the punching was remorseless. Frazier's face looked as if he had broken out in boils the size of fists. Ali was hit particularly hard on the hips and solar plexus as Frazier tried to cut the bigger man down to size. But Yank Durham and his assistant, the legendary Eddie

Futch, had given Frazier a winning game plan. They told their boxer to keep moving his head, to keep moving forward and to keep throwing punches, particularly hooks. Frazier did all this and more.

Ali hit Frazier with great shots but he could not stop the powerhouse. Ali, too, had lost that vital millisecond of speed that in the past would have taken him away from Frazier's heaviest punches. The two men traded blow for blow but Frazier finally won.

The bout came at a price for both men. They had created the richest prize fight in history, but they suffered. Frazier trudged away to his dressing room in great pain. Bundini Brown tried to console Ali in his dressing-room and shouted out in anger when representatives of the promoters tried to take away Ali's shorts and boots to auction as valuable memorabilia. 'They stay with the Champ. These are his war clothes,' he roared.

Ali's eyes were closed in pain. His hands were swollen and his jaw was numb. His doctor, Ferdie Pacheco, ordered him to hospital for X-rays but he had suffered no visible damage other than that caused by a severe pounding. Frazier, too, was taken to hospital. He had been suffering from high blood pressure before the fight. He was to stay in hospital for weeks.

But there was one scene in the defeated boxer's

dressing room that lives through the decades. Diana Ross, the singer, forced her way inside to talk to her hero. 'You The Champ. You won. You The Champ,' she said, in a distressed state.

'No, I am not,' Ali told her. 'I'm not The Champ any more.' Later he would tell the world: 'We been whupped. We all have to take defeats in life.'

But Smokin' Joe Frazier and Muhammad Ali would meet again. And again. Their rivalry was to be whipped by fury. It is a miracle both survived to tell the tale of the next two collisions.

ROUND 11

The Second Ogre

'This ain't nothing but another dramatic day in the life of Muhammad Ali.'
Muhammad Ali before the Foreman fight

HE looks cuddly now. The bald head shines under the television as he sells the hamburger grills that bear his name. He has found God, he is a grandfather and his chuckle is deep, throaty and friendly.

But once he was an ogre. Once he was the meanest, baddest man on the planet. Once he was George Foreman, champion of the world, and opponents trembled as they went out to face him. Foreman was so big, so strong that he tore open heavy boxing bags. He knocked down the formidable Joe Frazier six times in the time it takes to cook a hamburger on one of his grills. His record as he prepared to face Ali was 40 victories, 37 by knockout. Surely his meeting with Ali would be brief, even savagely routine? It was anything but. . .

The fight became another part of the Ali legend and another significant addition to boxing history. It was promoted by Don King, a former hustler from Houston who had served time in jail for killing a man in a brawl. King would use the Foreman-Ali fight to launch his career as one of the main players in boxing. King went on to dominate the sport, particularly the heavyweight division.

He extricated $10m from President Mobuto of Zaire to hold the Foreman-Ali fight in a stadium in Kinshasa. It is believed Zaire became the first country to sponsor a boxing match. Mobuto, a cruel and corrupt dictator, was using boxing to raise his profile in the world. He was a man of massive ego and murderous appetites. The heavyweight championship of the world was coming to Africa and the world's press resounded with stories of the black man coming home.

Ali was relaxed about the cultural surroundings. He was in Africa to box, to win back his title. He believed, too, that he had a great chance of beating Foreman. 'He is made for me,' he would tell reporters. He taunted

Foreman, calling him a monster who walked like The Mummy and had no boxing ability.

But sparring partners of Foreman told Ali a different story. One, Bossman Jones, had trained with Foreman for weeks and came to the Ali camp with tales of a fighter who could run up mountains, knock down good fighters with a single punch and box his way out of tight corners.

The fight, which became known as the Rumble in the Jungle, was made for September 24th, 1974, and Ali and his entourage flew to Zaire with a keen sense of anticipation. Ali was confident but he was also wary. He trained hard, soaking up punishment at the hands of heavy-hitting sparring partners. He watched Foreman spar and was surprised at what he witnessed.

'The champion was faster on his feet than I thought,' he recalled. So Ali dedicated himself to being in the best shape and his sparring partners were instructed to hit him hard and often. He was reaching his peak and ready to face a great challenge.

Then suddenly the fight was off. Foreman was cut over the right eye by a sparring partner. The bout was delayed for six weeks. But Ali kept training, kept his confidence up. Watched by Archie Moore, briefly his trainer and once the light heavyweight champion of the world, Ali shouted to his former mentor: 'Archie, go back and tell George that when we fight, the greatest miracle of all time will take place, the greatest miracle since the Resurrection of Christ, the biggest upset of all time. Bring that sucker in here! I will whip him now!'

But Moore was worried for Ali. He feared Foreman would destroy Ali, perhaps even kill him. He wrote his former protegé a letter. In it, he said: 'Even if Foreman misses with a punch, the whoosh of the air will lower the 90 degree temperature of Kinshasa very considerably.' He urged Ali to walk away from the fight, saying: 'The reason I am writing you this is that I do not want the blood of one of my talented ex-students on my otherwise clean and saintly hands.' He signed off: 'Yours, in prayer for your life.'

Moore's concern was shared by writers who had followed Ali throughout his career. Most looked at Foreman and saw a rock that The Greatest could not budge, never mind hurt. Ali had his doubts but they were not demoralising ones. He was assessing Foreman as a problem to be solved, not as one to avoid. He was buoyed, too, by the support of the people of Zaire.

The country had been a Belgian colony – named the Congo – and the inhabitants had been treated badly by their European rulers. Foreman made a big mistake when he walked down the steps from his plane with an Alsatian on a lead. The Zaireans immediately remembered that the repressive Belgian police also used Alsatian dogs to attack local inhabitants. Foreman, too, was viewed as surly and rude. He mumbled at press conferences and spent his time in the gym bashing a bag or a sparring partner.

Ali was different. His gym was like a vaudeville show. He was doing the work but he was also performing his verbal routines, making people laugh and applaud in sheer delight. His road work was accompanied by hordes of children running gleefully alongside him chanting: 'Ali-Bomaye,' an instruction for The Greatest to destroy Foreman.

The fight was an event not just for Zaire, not just for Africa, but for the world. Leon Gast captured the atmosphere in his Oscar-winning documentary 'When We Were Kings'. Norman Mailer, the famous American novelist, wrote a book, *The Fight*, about it. The world's press were at the ringside. Many had come with heavy hearts to see the end of Ali. They were to witness something else, something brilliant, something miraculous.

In the early hours of October 30th, 1974, Ali paced his dressing room, willing the fight to start. The scheduled time of the bout was 4am to suit television schedules in the USA but it also brought some relief from the baking heat of Zaire. It had not rained for weeks and Ali was already bathed in sweat as he danced in the dressing-room, flicking out his jab. As always, he said his prayers with his manager, Herbert Muhammad, son of Elijah, the one-time spiritual leader of the Nation of Islam. Typically of Ali, there were still reporters in the room and one asked: 'What goes through your mind before a fight?'

Ali answered: 'I think over what's at stake. I go over every preparation I have made. My roadwork was right. My diet was right. The way I trained was right. My sleep was right, my timing was right. For 30 days I timed my roadwork to take place at 4am so when I step into the ring at 4am it is going to be an exercise in the gym.'

Ali was ready. But Foreman felt he was, too. There was a strong sense of confidence in his dressing room. Ali's handlers were quieter, more apprehensive. 'They came into the dressing room as if they were walking behind a coffin. My coffin,' Ali remembered later.

Then it was time. Ali walked to the ring through cheering crowds. The moment of destiny had arrived for him. And Foreman.

Ali had to wait for the champion to come to the ring to join him. The Greatest took the acclaim of the crowd and then 'locked eyes' with Foreman 'like gunfighters in a Western'. The fight began in spectacular fashion. It was to end in even more dramatic circumstances. Ali told Foreman as they met to receive the referee's instructions: 'This sucker is in trouble.'

Ali opened the fight brightly, sticking his jab into Foreman's face. The crowd exploded but the champion was cutting down the ring, forcing Ali to expend energy in keeping away from him. The Greatest then decided to gamble. He chose to sink back on the ropes, drawing Foreman on. He was convinced that the giant would run out of strength if he continued to throw blows that were blocked by arms or taken on the hips. It was a stunning gamble. Ali was leaving himself open to the power of Foreman's blows. He enraged the champion by continuing to shout taunts at him. 'Is that the best you can do, sissy?' he asked as another Foreman haymaker landed.

There were later reports that Angelo Dundee had slackened the ropes pre-fight so Ali could lie on them, bending away from Foreman. Dundee always denied this, saying the strategy was much simpler. They wanted Ali to dance around the giant and pick him off with jabs.

Ali, in one instant, had changed the game plan. He felt he could not stay away from Foreman for 15 rounds. He drew the champ on. And then he slew him. Foreman had banged hard for seven rounds and when he came out for the eighth Ali felt his opponent's blows had become weaker. He knew he had the fight in his hands. A straight right to Foreman's jaw stopped the champion and suddenly, like a tree creaking and then falling, the ogre fell to the ground. He was counted out. Ali was champion of the world again. He had upset the odds again. He was The Greatest. Again.

Foremen trudged away from the ring with psychological wounds that would take years to heal. He was traumatised by defeat. Ali was swept back to the dressing-room in triumph. Moments after the fight ended, a rainstorm pounded down on the stadium. The sky was lit up by lightning and the rain formed swirling rivers. The drought had ended. It was a night for the spectacular, a night for the phenomenal.

ROUND 12

Good Guy, Bad Guy

'A man should never hit a woman.'
Muhammad Ali

HOW to judge Muhammad Ali? How to tally up the good points and the bad points and come to a definitive judgment on the man?

It is impossible. No man should be unbending in his assumptions of another and unswerving in his conclusions. It is, perhaps, safer to sift the evidence and say that Ali was capable of being good and bad. He is not the unblemished saint that his supporters claim. He is not the brutal villain that his detractors insist. He is, perhaps, an amalgam of both; in other words, all too human.

It must be noted that Ali was capable of cruelty both inside and outside the ring. It became obvious in his career that he could wound opponents with his words. These could be shrugged off but they did leave a painful legacy for some, particularly Joe Frazier. Smokin' Joe still bristles with anger at the way he was portrayed by his bitter rival.

But Ali's devastating one-two was to combine verbal assaults with the ability to torture opponents inside the ring.

Torture. It is an emotive word. Is it too strong? Ali could and would try to humiliate opponents by using his extraordinary skills to awful effect. He employed this as some kind of punishment, even as a warning to others not to cause him displeasure. If a boxer upset Ali in any way, The Greatest could simply be the meanest.

He was ruthlessly cruel in his treatment of Floyd Patterson, the former heavyweight champion. Patterson did not share Ali's Muslim views. He was a Roman Catholic who believed strongly that whites and blacks should live together. Patterson was never one to invite confrontation out of the ring. He was devout, polite and keen not to cause offence.

Ali derided Patterson as 'nothing but an Uncle Tom, a white man's negro'. Taunting Patterson over support for him among the establishment, he labelled his opponent 'The Black White Hope'. Patterson was, he emphasised, the kind of black man that the white race wanted to promote. His depiction of Patterson was clumsy and wrong. But Ali followed this up with a ruthless attitude towards his boxing opponent. He talked of developing a 'brutal instinct' and added, 'I want to see him cut and bruised, his ribs caved in and then knocked out.'

Patterson was punished in the fight on November 22nd, 1965, until he had to retire because of a back injury. Ali was merciless towards his opponent, seemingly keen to inflict pain rather than a knockout that would have saved Patterson excruciating punishment.

His fight against Ernie Terrell on February 6th, 1967, became infamous because of Ali's brutality. Terrell in pre-fight press conferences refused to call his opponent Muhammad Ali, referring constantly to Cassius Clay. Ali cut and shredded Terrell during the fight calling out: 'What's my name? What's my name?' One observer said: 'It was like a schoolboy pulling off the wings of a butterfly.' Terrell was beaten, even brutalised.

His attitude and behaviour towards women could be shameful, too. Ali has been married four times. He was a womaniser who was serially unfaithful. His first marriage to Sonji was annulled after he felt she had not embraced his Muslim faith. But Ali also admitted assaulting his first wife. 'She made vows and then broke them and that led to all sorts of quarrelling,' said Ali. 'One time, I slapped her. It was wrong. It's the only time I did something like that, and after I slapped her I felt sorrier than she did. It hurt me more than it hurt her. I was young, 22 years old, and she was doing things against my religion, but that's no excuse. A man should never hit a woman.'

Three more marriages followed. Ali married 17-year-old Belinda Boyd on August 17th, 1967. But Ali then began an affair with Veronica Porsche, a model, in 1975, and the marriage ended two years later. Ali and Veronica married and then were later divorced in 1986 and in November of that year Ali married Yolanda Ali.

They live happily together now but it must be noted that Ali's womanising had an effect on those around him and cost him at least one marriage.

It must be stressed, however, that Ali had a good side and this has become stronger with maturity. He had the ability to be extremely kind to people, particularly those who were downtrodden or suffering. One friend recalled Ali visiting a women's prison. 'He had the gift of making these women feel they were special,' said the friend.

Ali, too, was famous for giving money away. He would walk down a street with his entourage and pass out dollar bills to anyone he felt needed them. More than one beggar on the streets would look down at his cup and stare in disbelief as he saw it crammed with dollars. George Chuvalo, a one-time opponent in the ring, was also grateful to The Greatest for speaking at his testimonial without asking for expenses or a fee. 'He simply would not take a penny,' said Chuvalo. 'He is a man of integrity with a good heart.'

Aspiring boxers would travel to Ali's home and be warned against pursuing the most unforgiving of trades with most being given money to help them return home.

Ali was most generous with children and children's charities. And he had the ability to connect with people, to make the most damaged feel full of worth. 'He would walk into the ghetto and just talk to people,' said Jim Brown, the American footballer who became an actor. 'His greatest attribute was, no matter how famous he was, he loved every person he saw.'

Ali was kind, perhaps too kind, to his huge entourage. Most fleeced Ali of money. Some repaid him with kind words. Ralph Thornton, one of the army of helpers, said: 'Ali did more than pay me. He did more for me than anybody in my family ever did. He took me places I would never have been able to go to on my own. We went first class and lived first class. As far as my life is concerned, Ali opened up the world.'

The Greatest was also the most accessible of champions. When he was training at his camp in Deer Lake, Pennsylvania, tourists and other sightseers would venture up to the compound. At first they put up a rope to deter these fans, but Ali tore it down. He loved performing in front of people and made time for every visit, much to the annoyance of many in his camp.

The champion could also have a life-changing effect on those he met. Many were moved by his kindnesses. Many were grateful for the dollars he pressed in their hands. But he could also change attitudes. Pat Patterson, Ali's security officer, was never afraid to use violence to restore what he believed was order. 'With Ali I realised it was more important to be a peace officer, that people needed help. He taught me to take time and listen to people,' he said.

The Greatest, too, retained his ability of surprising with his gestures. The rebel who would not serve in Vietnam took a $100,000 hit by giving 2000 tickets to American soldiers serving in Germany for a fight with Richard Dunn. 'I didn't go because of my religion, they are just doing their job,' he said.

Many old opponents found Ali could be kind out of the ring. Ken Norton, one of his great adversaries, was injured in a car crash in 1986. He woke up in hospital to be entertained by Ali doing magic tricks.

Ali has become more mellow, with his bad side rarely now in evidence. Kris Kristofferson, the singer and actor, who has spent time with Ali both as a friend and as an artist, once said: 'The first thing that struck me about Muhammad was his genuine love for everybody we met. People were always asking him to sign autographs and pose for pictures and he gave everyone what they wanted.'

Ali has dealt out the bad; he now specialises in dealing out the good. He has matured as person, survived as a human being. But his very existence was given its strongest test on a clammy Manila morning.

ROUND 13
Thrilla, Chiller, Killer

'Frazier was a fighter who made me feel
he was taking me to the door of death.'
Muhammad Ali

THEY had to fight again. It was their fate, their destiny, maybe even their tragedy. Thirty-five months after Joe Frazier had won in Madison Square Garden, the two faced up for what now is almost a forgotten fight. It lacked the freshness of Ali-Frazier I and it was mercifully deprived of the gory horror of Ali-Frazier III but it was still tough, uncompromising and controversial.

They routinely traded insults before walking into the ring again at Madison Square Garden on January 28th, 1974. There was even a pre-match fight on television when Ali and Frazier grappled after an argument about who had spent longest in hospital after their first clash.

'Everyone knows I was in the hospital for 10 minutes,' said Ali to Frazier on a chat show five days before the fight. 'You were in the hospital for three weeks. You are ignorant Joe.'

Frazier stood up and loomed over Ali and the two boxers grabbed each other. 'The fight was real,' said one observer. Boxing authorities later fined them $5000 each.

The grapple in the studio could be called a draw but the fight in Madison Square Garden was Ali's triumph. He won a decision after 12 rounds although Frazier, and trainer Eddie Futch, were not pleased at the officiating. They accused Tony Perez, the referee, of allowing Ali to pull Frazier's head into his chest, thus depriving Smokin' Joe of room to swing his big hooks.

Frazier was not pleased at the judges, either. 'It wasn't the first and for damn sure it wouldn't be the last time Clay got a gift from the judges,' he said later. 'But I didn't make a big fuss about the decision. That wasn't my way. I was no crybaby like Clay after the first one, talking his bull and trying to persuade folks he didn't get his ass kicked. In boxing you take the good and the bad and push on.'

The score was 1-1. Frazier had taken the first fight,

Ali had won the second. There had to be a third but the world had to wait until October 1st, 1975, for the decider. It was always going to happen. Frazier and Ali constantly sought each other out even after two dramatic fights. They were true rivals. 'I hate him,' said Frazier. 'I want him again.' Ali was more restrained but equally firm: 'I think we should do it again. I'm not going to duck Joe. I'll give him all the chances he wants.'

The desire they had to face each other was evident in the build-up to what became known as the Thrilla in Manila. 'I want you like a hog wants slop,' Frazier told Ali in eager anticipation.

But the days before the event were also marked by two incidents that did Ali's reputation no favours. First, Ali had taken his mistress, Veronica Porche to the Phillippines, instead of his wife, Belinda. Veronica was paraded in front of the world's press, even attending a reception given by President Ferdinand Marcos. It was to be the final humiliation for Belinda who ended the marriage soon after.

Second, Ali was brutal in his depiction of Frazier. He brought out a small, toy gorilla and called it 'Joe'. He told pressmen and watching fans how ugly and stupid Frazier was. He made up one of his rhymes.

It will be a killer
And a chiller
And a thrilla
When I get the gorilla
In Manila

Frazier was enraged. His rising anger was quietly but bitterly expressed. 'There will come a moment. . . and he's going to remember what it is like to be in [the ring] with me, how hard and long that night is going to be,' he said.

That night came in a ring in Quezon City, six miles outside Manila. It was one of the most ferocious, draining and spectacularly brutal fights ever witnessed. In the clammy, suffocating air of the Philippines, both men felt they were gasping their last breath. Two great champions gave everything. This was more than a world title fight. This was more than a sporting contest. 'They were fighting for the championship of each other,' said journalist Jerry Izenberg.

The story of the fight is simple to relate, though its sheer drama can only be glimpsed by watching a video of the contest. Ali won the early rounds, Frazier took command in the middle of the fight, and then Ali came back strongly at the end.

But no man took a step back. There were gasps in the crowd at the sheer ferocity of the action. Pressmen with the experience of watching hundreds of bouts, thousands of rounds, could not believe what was happening in front of their eyes. Ali, in the later rounds, hammered Frazier with unanswered blows to the head. He could not believe Frazier would not go down.

Smokin' Joe had been doused by Foreman but he would not fall before Ali. 'They told me Joe Frazier was washed up. They lied,' said a bewildered champion. Frazier, too, had been stunned by Ali's resilience as he battered him with hooks. 'He had an amazing chin,' he would later say grudgingly of his detested foe.

The fight seemed destined to go the full distance, forcing the judges to make a decision on who had won a titanic contest. But, late in the fight, Ali took control. Frazier's face became a mass of bumps. The areas surrounding his eyes became grotesquely swollen. It became obvious that Frazier simply could not see.

Eddie Futch, Frazier's trainer, was deeply concerned. At the end of the 13th round, he considered throwing in the towel and preventing his boxer from going back out to face punishment he could not dodge. But he allowed Frazier one more round. At the end of the 14th round, however, the trainer feared he could have Frazier's death on his hands. As his boxer stumbled back to his corner, bloodied but defiant, Futch made the decision. Frazier protested with all the might his

exhausted body and mind could summon. But Futch
told him: 'Sit down, son. It's over, but no one will ever
forget what you did here tonight.'

In the other corner, Ali was drained, desperately ill.
He had spoken to himself throughout the fight about
'going down to the well once more', meaning he was
trying to summon up reserves from his deepest being.
But he knew he was being pushed to the extremes. 'The
closest thing to dying I know,' he later said of the bout.
He also added: 'Frazier was a fighter who made me feel
he was taking me to the door of death.'

On that day in Quezon City, he looked across the
ring as he braced himself for the final round and saw
his most enduring rival slumped on a stool. 'His face
was a gory mass, his lips were cut in a dozen places,
there were lumps all over his head and face,' Ali recalled.
And then he saw that Frazier was not going to come
out. It was over. Ali collapsed in exhaustion.

Angelo Dundee, his trainer, said: 'It was a brutal fight.
Both guys ran out of gas but my guy had an extra tank.'
But even that was almost drained.

Ferdie Pacheco, the doctor to The Greatest, said: 'Ali
was badly beaten up. It took about 24 hours for his
brain to recuperate, for his thought processes to become
complete.' Ali made the winner's reception but he looked
as if he had been hit by a car. Several times.

Mark Kram, a journalist who saw Frazier immediately after the fight, reported that the boxer could not see, his eyes were slits. Frazier told him: 'Man I hit him with punches that'd bring down the walls of a city. Lawdy, Lawdy, he's a great champion.' Then he limped to the reception. His face was a mass of wounds but he did not want the world to know how much he hurt. He did not want it said that he could not leave his bed.

Ali, too, was hurting. Of the immediate aftermath to the fight, he said: 'I got enough strength to get back to the dressing room and laid on my couch. Every bone felt as though it has been smashed by a crowbar.' He was gracious to Frazier at the reception but his opponent could not forgive.

'It wasn't just a fight. It was me and him. Not a fight,' said Frazier, reflecting on the great rivalry. The two boxers had endured three bouts comprised of 42 bloody, awful rounds.

The impact had been profound. 'The fights with Frazier had done true damage to Ali and Manila had been the last, life-altering choice of his long, long trip in a game where longevity is a killer,' wrote Mark Kram. Frazier later brutally referred to Ali as 'damaged goods', claiming that his fights with The Greatest had inflicted the health problems that the champion was to suffer in later life.

Ali, feeling the pain of Manila, immediately reflected: 'Everything in me is aflame. This is it for me. It's over.' But there was still more drama and tragedy to come for Ali in the ring.

ROUND 14

The Long Goodbye

'Father Time caught up with me.'
                           Muhammad Ali

THERE was pain for Ali after Manila, there was defeat too. And there was glory and redemption. But there were also the beatings and the slide to retirement. He was older, slower. But he was no less defiant. He would not quit.

Manila would have been the perfect moment to leave the stage but The Greatest's timing deserted him. He fought Jean-Pierre Coopman, a shambling Belgian sculptor. He won easily in five rounds. He battled Jimmy Young over 15 rounds. It was untidy and showed Ali was failing. Richard Dunn was dismissed easily in five rounds. But Ali's next tests would show he was no longer the boxer of old. Ali defeated Ken Norton on a decision over 15 rounds but there were protests that the champion was very lucky. Alfredo Evangelista took him to another exhausting 15 rounds. 'In my Sonny Liston days, when I was young, I would have eaten Evangelista up,' said The Greatest, 'I can't do it any more.'

But still he fought on.

Earnie Shavers, one of the hardest hitters ever, then showed the strength of Ali's chin and the champ's incredible desire and will not to be beaten. Ali won a close decision in a bruising encounter.

Teddy Brenner, matchmaker at Madison Square Garden, said: 'As long as I am here, Madison Square Garden will never make Ali an offer to fight again. This is a young man's game. Ali is 35, he has half his life ahead of him. Why take chances. There is nothing more for him to prove. I don't want him to come to me some day and say: "What's your name?"' The trick in boxing is to get out at the right time and the 15th round last night was the right time for Ali.'

But still he went on.

The night of February 15th, 1978, in the Las Vegas Hilton was a moment of reckoning. Ali lost to Leon Spinks over 15 rounds. It was an abject performance.

Ali was a shadow of his great self. And he knew it. 'Of all the fights I lost, losing to Spinks hurt the most. It was my fault. Leon did the best he could, but it was embarrassing that someone with so little fighting skills could beat me. I didn't train right, I gave away the first six rounds, figuring he'd tire out, and it turned out I got tired. It was embarrassing.'

Spinks, an Olympic gold medallist in 1976 in Montreal at light heavyweight, hit Ali during the fight and hit the mark after it. 'I got 12 years on Ali. Let's face it. He's an old man.'

The old man was philosophical. 'We all lose in life. We all have losses, what you have to do is keep living, overcome these losses and come back,' he said. This is a good way to live life. It is not a healthy way to maintain a boxing career.

But Ali went on.

And, being The Greatest, he triumphed spectacularly. On the night of September 15th, 1978, in the Super-dome in New Orleans, Ali became the world heavyweight champion for the third time. He defeated Spinks over 15 rounds.

'This will be my Third Coming,' said Ali before the fight. He was right. 'I've lasted longer than the Beatles and the Supremes,' he said. 'Now it is just me and the

Rolling Stones.' It was a great triumph but the clamour and the hype could not disguise the reality. Ali was the champion again but Spinks had been poor in the bout, perhaps feeling the strains of a frenetic lifestyle.

The danger was that Ali would take this victory as a sign of his immortality. But he was flawed, weaker and surely someone would expose these failings. He seemed to recognise this by announcing his retirement on September 6th, 1979.

But still he went on.

It was a decision that was to be proved dangerously, painfully wrong. Ali faced Larry Holmes in Las Vegas on October 2nd, 1980. He was 38 years old and facing a former sparring partner. Holmes was strong, skilful and motivated. He was also world champion, having taken the title after Ali had retired. There were genuine concerns for Ali's well-being against the formidable Holmes. Ferdie Pacheco warned: 'When old talents fail, all that is left is guile, experience, cunning and will – I know Ali has stepped into his past. His body is dead.'

Ali was now suffering from a tingling in his hands and his speech was becoming slurred. But still he went on, stepping into the ring to face Holmes. The champion loved Ali but this was his chance at glory. A boxing ring is a dangerous place to be merciful. 'I'm going to hurt Ali,' he said. 'This is something I have never wanted to do. He's got to be down on his knees before I look to the referee to help him. I'm fighting for Larry Holmes' identity.'

An ageing fighter faced an accomplished, inspired champion. There could only be one outcome. 'I thought they should have stopped it in the sixth round,' said Richie Giacametti, Holmes' trainer. 'After that, there was no point in going on.' Holmes said at one point during the beating: 'Doesn't everyone realise I am hitting him at will.' But still it went on.

Dave Kindred, a reporter with the *Washington Post*, remembered: 'I sat next to Herbert Muhammad [Ali's manager] during the fight and he never said a word. Mostly, he just hung his head and looked as if he was in pain.' The terrible assault ended after the 10th round. 'Herbert signalled to someone. He shook his head and Angelo [Dundee] stopped it.' Dundee told referee Richard Greene: 'That's all.' Bundini Brown, Ali's second, pleaded: 'One more round.' But Dundee swore at him and then said: 'I'm the chief second. The ball game is over.'

It was the only decision to make. Even a warrior like Ali had to agree with it, however reluctantly. 'I didn't want Angelo to stop it,' he said. 'I wanted to go 15 rounds. But I guess what he did was right because if it had gone on, maybe I would have got hurt more.'

After the fight, Holmes went to Ali's room. He told his hero: 'You're still The Greatest. I love you.' But Ali was still defiant. 'I do not think it was a matter of age,' he said, though he had dyed his grey hair black before the fight. 'I think I became dehydrated by dieting and training too hard.'

Ferdie Pacheco, though, was severely honest in his assessment. 'Ali was like a vain actress who's 40 and wants to look 20 again. Maybe he looked young, but he was past his age in terms of physical condition.'

But still he went on.

The Greatest, one of the most sublime boxers to grace the ring, was then involved in a farce. He faced Trevor Berbick, a limited boxer, on December 11th, 1981, in Nassau, in the Bahamas. The show started two hours late because the promoters could not find a key for the front gate of the baseball field where the fight was to be held. Then the organisers discovered they had only two pairs of gloves for the entire support bouts. Then no bell could be found so the officials had to use a cowbell. But finally the main event proceeded.

Every fan of Ali wished it had not. Again, The Greatest was hit at will, but this time by an opponent far inferior to Holmes. He lost a unanimous decision over 10 rounds. It was a defeat that finally convinced Ali that he could no longer operate in the ring. 'Father Time caught up with me,' he said. 'I'm finished. For the first time I feel old. I know it is the end. I am not crazy. We all lose sometimes. We all grow old.'

But he was wonderfully, brilliantly defiant. The ego shone on. 'At least, I didn't go down,' he said, referring to his ability to stay on his feet during the final onslaughts. 'No picture of me on the floor, no pictures of me falling through the ropes, no broken teeth, no blood. I'm happy I am still pretty.'

But he was damaged. The Parkinson's syndrome was already evident. It would begin to take an increasing toll on his health and limit his life. The Greatest limped away, rather than being carried high on triumph. The will that forced him through the worst of Frazier's blows, the courage that disarmed Liston and then confounded Foreman had been used to inflict damage on Ali himself. He was constitutionally unable to give up.

The decision should not have been left to him. But, finally, Ali had to step out of the ring for the last time. He was bruised and hurt. He was lonely and his ego missed the glory and the sheer excitement of the ring.

But still he went on. He had the rest of his life to lead.

ROUND 15
The Final Round

'I sign my name, we eat.'
Muhammad Ali

THE Greatest sits, hands trembling, and puts his name on boxing memorabilia. The Ali name has a resonance, a value. It is put on a pair of $20 gloves and enhances its value by ten times, twenty times, whatever someone wants to pay at auction. A $15 poster gains an extra zero, maybe two, by the application of an Ali scrawl.

The man remains a legend. People pay to come as close as they can to that sort of hero. Ali has cause to be grateful for that phenomenon.

His health and wealth have all but disappeared. It is

his physical condition that has caused the most controversy. There are those who say he is 'punch drunk'. They claim he took too many blows and is suffering the consequences. He displays the symptoms of Parkinson's syndrome: a tremor, a slowness of movement, a rigidity of muscles, including muscles used in speech, and difficulty in balance.

Those visiting Ali now note that The Greatest talks very slowly in a mumble. He is prone to falling asleep suddenly, though his sense of mischief survives. Sometimes he seems to fall asleep, only to cock open an eye slyly and murmur 'gotcha' at his companion.

His life outside boxing has been marked by the redemption offered by the Supreme Court when they cleared him of all charges regarding his refusal to serve in the army. He also became a loved figure in the United States and there was no more poignant sight than a visibly ailing Muhammad Ali lighting the torch for the 1996 Olympics in Atlanta.

But Ali fought through the terms of seven presidents and he paid the price for this longevity and for his increasing tendency to be hit, indeed to allow himself to be hit. Ali in later years used to invite sparring partners to batter him persistently as if to toughen himself up for fights. He also took ferocious blows in fights. The battles against Frazier were brutal, the collision with George Foreman jarred bone and brain and other fights must have inflicted damage. History will remember Ali as a classy fighter, a sleek mover. He was, though, a warrior who could take the blows and come back for more. He broke his jaw against Ken Norton and would not quit. He was pummelled by Foreman and would not quit. He was decked by Frazier and would not quit. No one could ever accuse Ali of not having what fight fans call heart. But was this defiance a trait that caused awful damage down the line?

Ferdie Pacheco, his doctor, has no doubts. 'Athletes get old early,' said Pacheco, who left the Ali camp when he felt the boxer was going on too long. 'If I had to pick a spot to tell him: "You've got all your marbles, but don't go on anymore", no question it would have been after Frazier [in Manila]. That is when it really started to fall apart. He began to take beatings, not just in fights but in the gym.'

If it is difficult to be precise about if and when boxing induced the Parkinson's syndrome, it is impossible to trace just where all Ali's money has gone. There are reports that he has some investments in property and trust funds and he is far from starving but it is telling that he indulges so readily in the autograph-writing sessions. Ali was a money-making machine but he misfired when it came to retaining much of it. He fought for astonishing multi-million dollar purses against a succession of fighters. But much of the money was squandered, embezzled or just given away.

Herbert Muhammad, Ali's manager, is believed to have taken 50% of takings as his proprietorial due. Angelo Dundee received a percentage. And then there was the entourage. Ali could travel with more than 50 people in tow. He had trainers, cooks, security guards, masseurs, sparring partners and those for whom there seemed to be no defined role. They all travelled first class, stayed in first-class hotels and lived first-class lives. Ali once summoned his travelling army for a dressing down in a German hotel suite after seeing how the bill for his stay was soaring. There were people ordering multiple steaks, phoning long-distance to the United States on a regular basis and charging a multitude of extras to Ali's account.

His anger did not last long, however. Ali was always tough in the ring and regularly gentle outside it. Seeing the crestfallen faces of his friends, he staunched his angry flow and merely told them to be more careful when spending in future.

There were attempts from outsiders to help Ali keep his money but they were doomed to failure. A group of bankers decided that the champion's financial affairs were in such a dire state something had to be done. One exasperated banker told him: 'You act like you want to prove you have a constitutional right to go broke.'

Ali would endorse such junk that his name would become tarnished. He failed to cash in with advertising and endorsements that would be properly remunerative. Ali rarely complains but there is a wistfulness in one comment. 'Sometimes I wish I had gone to college,' he said. 'I could have done more if I had gotten a better education.' This partly refers to his financial disasters. An educated Ali may have been more vigilant in guarding his investments, protecting his future.

But perhaps not.

Ali's carelessness with money reflected much of his personality. He was interested in much more than a dollar bill. He was always searching for some sort of calmness, some sort of certainty about the purpose of life. He has lost money and a significant proportion of his health. But he has found peace. Those who know Ali best say The Greatest has become more spiritual and introspective as he has aged.

Pacheco, the doctor who is convinced that boxing damaged Ali's health irreparably, believes his friend has found something else. 'Luckily he has what all of us would like to have; spiritual serenity,' he said. 'He is the only guy I know who has got it. He's got total peace of mind because he has convinced himself that here is not where it is at. Heaven is where it is at. And he's working hard to get there, and he has the absolute knowledge that he is going.'

He and his fourth wife, Lonnie, live quietly, with Ali only venturing out to the odd function, such as the inauguration of President Barack Obama. He lives in observance of his faith. He prays and meditates. He still lights up at old memories and enjoys showing his magic tricks to visitors, particularly young children.

'I don't want anyone to feel sorry for me because I had a good life before and I am having a good life now,' he once said. He is aware of his failing health, his shaking hands and his slow speech. He does not suffer from self-pity, though. 'God's showing me I'm just a man like everyone else.' A man in all his frailty and faults. But a hero, too, in his deeds and triumphs.

BIBLIOGRAPHY

Muhammad Ali: His Life and Times Thomas Hauser (Robson Books, 2004)

McIlvanney on Boxing Hugh McIlvanney (Mainstream, 1997)

The Greatest: My Own Story with Richard Durham (Random House, 1975)

King of the World David Remnick (Random House, 1998)

Ghosts of Manila Mark Kram (HarperCollins, 2002)

The Fight Norman Mailer (Penguin Classics, 2000)

Muhammad Ali's Greatest Fight: Cassius Clay v The United States of America Howard Bingham and Max Wallace (Robson, 2004)

My View from the Corner: A Life in Boxing Angelo Dundee (McGraw Hill, 2009)

Night Train: A Biography of Sonny Liston Nick Tosches (Hamish Hamilton, 2000)

Liston and Ali: The Ugly Bear and the Boy Who Would be King Bob Mee (Mainstream, 2010)

Smokin' Joe, The Autobiography (Macmillan, 1996)

By George, The Autobiography of George Foreman
(Joel Engel - Easton Press, 1995)

The Autobiography of Malcolm X (Penguin Classics,
2001)

Other titles in the
INSPIRATIONS series

Charles Dickens

Hard Times and Great Expectations

Alan Taylor

From his early twenties Charles Dickens was the world's most celebrated novelist. Nor since his death in 1870 has much changed. His books, such as *Great Expectations*, *David Copperfield* and *Oliver Twist*, are still read with admiration and awe, while characters like Squeers and Fagan, Pickwick and Gradgrind, remain as familiar as when they were first encountered. Meanwhile, Dickens' own life, as Alan Taylor relates in this short but perfectly-formed biography, was as fascinating and colourful as any of those he invented.

ISBN:	978 1 906134 67 9
classification:	biography
cover price:	£5.99 paperback
extent:	128 pages, colour cover with flaps
size:	178 x 111mm

www.argyllpublishing.co.uk

John Lennon

the story of the original Beatle

Chris Dolan

John Lennon's life is one of the best known stories in the whole of popular culture. . . and yet there is always an unknown element to his character and his work.

Arguably no other composer or performer had such a profound impact on people. And few other public figures of the last century, from any walk of life, have had so many seemingly separate existences – pop star, spokesman, tragic victim, madman, jester – and genius.

Chris Dolan captures the essence of John Lennon's creative life and work. From a painful and bewildering Liverpool childhood to world renown, his and his fellow Beatles' sheer musicianship and inventiveness, imagination, skill and ambition are awesome. Lennon's life is an inspiration.

ISBN: 978 1 906134 68 6
classification: biography
cover price: £5.99 paperback
extent: 128 pages, colour cover with flaps
size: 178 x 111mm
www.argyllpublishing.co.uk

J K Rowling

the mystery of fiction

Lindsey Fraser

J K Rowling's story is almost as magical as her books. The day she wrote the name Harry Potter on a page she changed not just her own unhappy life but that of millions of readers. Harry Potter and his friends turned Rowling into one of the richest and most influential women in the world. So who is she, and where did her ideas come from? Lindsey Fraser tells the remarkable tale that began one day on a train, when Rowling had forgotten to pack a pen. . .

ISBN: 978 1 906134 69 3
classification: biography
cover price: £5.99 paperback
extent: 128 pages, colour cover with flaps
size: 178 x 111mm
www.argyllpublishing.co.uk

Nelson Mandela

Robben Island to Rainbow Nation

Marian Pallister

Fairness, equality, leadership and justice had been
values instilled in prisoner 46664 from his earliest
years among his Xhosa people. Nelson Mandela
had been a leading figure in the struggle for
change in the apartheid state of South Africa. That
is why he was in one of the toughest prisons in the
world. Robben Island's maximum security prison,
built to house political prisoners, offered no escape
route. The treatment was brutal and numbers came
before names. Yet, more than four decades after
his imprisonment the name Mandela continues to
be an inspiration in the on-going struggle to create
a better world.

ISBN: 978 1 906134 52 5
classification: biography
cover price: £5.99 paperback
extent: 128 pages, colour cover with flaps
size: 178 x 111mm
www.argyllpublishing.co.uk